BRAZIL
State and Struggle

Latin America Bureau
Research and action on Latin America

First published in Great Britain in 1982 by

Latin America Bureau (Research and Action) Ltd,
1 Amwell Street, London EC1R 1UL.

Copyright © Latin America Bureau (Research and Action) Ltd, 1982.
ISBN 0 906156 16 5

Written by Bernardo Kucinski
Editing and additional writing by David Fig and Sue Branford
Translation and editing assistance by Nick Terdry and Iain Bruce
Design by Jan Brown Designs
Cover photo by Abel Lagos
Maps by Michael Green
Typeset, printed and bound by Russell Press Ltd, Nottingham
Trade Distribution in UK by Third World Publications

Contents

Introduction

Abertura is a word which has no precise equivalent in English, but in the context of today's Brazil we need to understand its meaning. It refers to moves by the Brazilian military dictatorship to 'open up' or 'widen' the process of political participation in the country's affairs. The dictatorship has had to take account of recent developments: a severe economic crisis with no short-term solution and the growth of an independent workers' movement with substantial industrial and political muscle. It is also eager to lose its international reputation as a repressive violator of human rights.

Yet when we examine the dictatorship's response and assess the practical results of *abertura,* we see that the decisive factor at all times has been the dictatorship's desire to control the process. All concessions to the demands of the political opposition, for instance, have been hedged with restrictions and limitations. A glaring example is the November 1982 elections. Although new parties have been allowed to compete for office, electoral regulations have been freely manipulated so as to minimize the possibility of an opposition victory.

Alliances between parties are forbidden, voting is weighted against those regions in which the opposition's strength is concentrated, and to be allowed to run, new parties must put up candidates in every part of Brazil. To cap it all, the ballot forms have deliberately been designed to confuse voters and cause a high rate of annulled votes. That the regime should consider such an outcome conducive to its interests raises doubts about its proclaimed enthusiasm for democracy. That it had to over-rule the Supreme Electoral Tribunal, by using non-constitutional powers, in order to get its ballot paper 'approved' surely confirms such doubts.

Despite these machinations, some concessions have been made in the sphere of party politics. However, the dictatorship was unwilling to concede anything in other spheres. The advances which undoubtedly occurred in these spheres were the result of the initiatives of the industrial working class.

Since 1978 one of the outstanding features of the industrial scene has been the workers' widespread use of the strike weapon. This was not because the authorities conceded this right after violently suppressing it in the previous ten years, but because the authorities decided that they could contain the labour movement by appearing to concede to some of its demands.

In practice the regime has demonstrated clearly that *abertura* was not intended for the workers. The labour code drafted in the 1930s in emulation of Mussolini's corporatism is still in force, and all kinds of obstacles hinder workers' attempts to organize freely and independently of the state. Many strikes are declared illegal and union leaders have been put on trial on serious national security charges for organizing them. Strikers have been harassed and even shot by the police. Elected trade union officials have been summarily replaced by state appointees. Small wonder that the workers dismiss *abertura* as a charade. In the words of Luís Inácio da Silva (Lula), a prominent trade union leader:

The authorities continue to talk about *abertura*. They say they are building a democracy. Only they do not fool us any more: *abertura* is the new name they have given to the repression of the workers.

These sentiments are widely shared inside the labour movement, and are echoed by trade unionist Waldemar Rossi in the interview which appears later in this book.

Again, for the millions living in the countryside, *abertura* has meant little direct change. Massive social and economic inequality persists, underlining the urgent need for radical land reform. Indeed, as this Special Brief highlights, repression in the interior has intensified as the state protects large landholders from popular and church initiatives for a just form of land distribution. Drought, evictions, and the substitution by agribusiness of staple foodstuffs for more profitable commodities like soya have only added to the misery of small farmers and the rural landless.

If the reality of *abertura* is no more than a limited and skewed extension of the electoral system, we need to guard ourselves against loose usage of the concept. On the one hand the dictatorship has employed the concept ideologically, to justify the maintenance of the existing power structure under new and more difficult conditions. In giving the regime credit for the extension of political participation, many Brazilians and outside observers may overlook the severe limitations placed on this process, and be deluded that Brazil has entered a new phase of democratization. The delusion may serve to reconcile many potential opponents with the regime, extending the 'legitimacy' of the dictatorship. Another danger in misconstruing *abertura* is to imagine that there has been an end to overt forms of repression; instead we need to chart how the repression has continued, and to unmask the reality behind the ideological concept of *abertura*.

In order to undertake this task, we have embarked on an exploration of Brazilian history since the downfall of the 'Old Republic' in 1930. Our focus has been upon the Brazilian state, through an analysis of the different social forces which have excercized state power, and the challenges which have been presented to that power. Of crucial importance is the political role of the military in acting as power-brokers throughout this time, and in their assuming full control of the state since 1964.

The worldwide economic depression at the end of the 1920s created conditions in Brazil for local industrialization. At the political level this phase was dominated by the figure of Getúlio Vargas. Installed in power in 1930, he instituted a dictatorship between 1937-45, and guided the first decade of post-war democracy, even resuming the presidency in 1950 until his suicide in 1954. Among his strong supporters was João Goulart, vice-president between 1956-61, and president from 1961-64. Thus the legacy of Vargas persisted until the establishment of the military dictatorship, and many acknowledge a degree of continuity up to the present time.

Two chapters are devoted to the above; the first examines the period from 1930-45, and the second the democratic phase between 1945-64. The following four chapters cover the military dictatorship, one devoted to its first decade, two to the Geisel presidency, and the final one to the current regime under Figueiredo. In each we examine the particular form of the regime, the coalition of forces in power, and the response of the popular movement, comprising the organizations of workers, peasants, students, the marginalized, and often the church. The 'struggle' in the book's title is seen to be that between the ruling groups and the popular movement.

This struggle has entered a new phase since the late 1970s with the re-emergence of the working class as a political force, in response to attempts by the employers to shift the burden of the current economic crisis onto its shoulders. In many other developing countries, industrial workers have become a relatively privileged stratum of society, trading job security for an amenable attitude towards the state. But in Brazil, most workers' living standards have been diminished and their opposition to the ruling groups has intensified.

This opposition has taken three forms: an *economic* struggle on an industrial level in which huge strikes have been organized against employers; a *political* struggle against the dictatorship which has drawn in a whole range of community-based, church and women's organisations; and an *internal* struggle for the establishment of a united democratic trade union movement independent of state interference and manipulation.

This process of struggle is crucial in the building of a democratic future for Brazil and in putting an end to the heavy burden of exploitation and inequality borne by the majority of its inhabitants. It also serves as an inspiration to similar struggles elsewhere. As such it demands our support and solidarity, to which it is hoped this book will serve as a modest contribution.

David Fig
Latin American Bureau

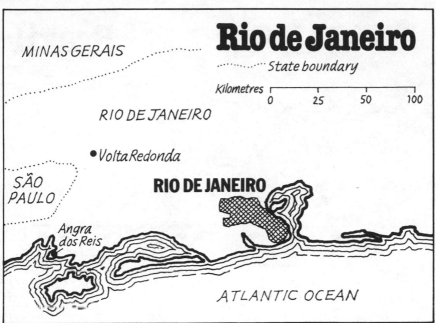

Rio de Janeiro

MINAS GERAIS

······· State boundary

Kilometres |—————————————————————|
0   25   50   100

RIO DE JANEIRO

• Volta Redonda

RIO DE JANEIRO

SÃO PAULO

Angra dos Reis

ATLANTIC OCEAN

São Paulo

Kilometres |—————————————————————|
0   25   50   100

SÃO PAULO

• Sorocaba

SÃO PAULO

Osasco •

• São Caetano do Sul

Diadema •

• Santo André

• São Bernardo do Campo

ATLANTIC OCEAN

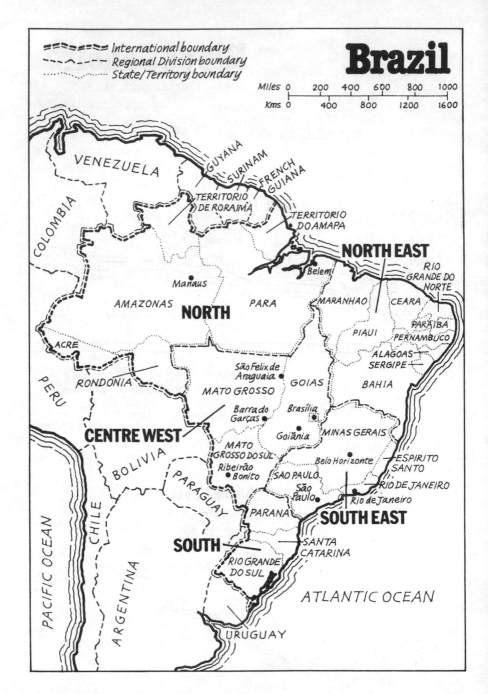

Brazil

International boundary
Regional Division boundary
State/Territory boundary

Miles 0   200   400   600   800   1000
Kms 0   400   800   1200 1600

PACIFIC OCEAN

VENEZUELA

COLOMBIA

GUYANA

SURINAM

FRENCH GUIANA

TERRITORIO DE RORAIMA

TERRITORIO DO AMAPA

NORTH EAST

RIO GRANDE DO NORTE

Belem

Manaus

AMAZONAS

PARA

MARANHAO

CEARA

NORTH

PIAUI

PARAIBA

PERNAMBUCO

ACRE

ALAGOAS

SERGIPE

PERU

RONDONIA

São Felix de Araguaia

MATO GROSSO

GOIAS

BAHIA

Barra do Garças

Brasília

CENTRE WEST

BOLIVIA

MATO GROSSO DO SUL

Goiânia

MINAS GERAIS

Belo Horizonte

ESPIRITO SANTO

Ribeirão Bonito

SAO PAULO

RIO DE JANEIRO

PARAGUAY

São Paulo

Rio de Janeiro

PARANA

SOUTH EAST

CHILE

SOUTH

SANTA CATARINA

RIO GRANDE DO SUL

ARGENTINA

ATLANTIC OCEAN

URUGUAY

vi

1 Brazil in Brief

Statistics

Area 8,511,965km^2 = 3,286,369 sq miles
(35 times the size of the UK)

Population Total 119,070,865 (1980)

Growth 2.8% (annual average rate 1970-80)

Urban 1940: 36%
1950: 38%
1960: 44%
1970: 56%
1980: 68%

Principal Cities (1980)
São Paulo 8.5 million
Rio de Janeiro 5.0 million
Belo Horizonte 1.8 million
Salvador 1.5 million
Fortaleza 1.3 million
Recife 1.2 million
Porto Alegre 1.125 million
Brasília 1.117 million

The People Origins European 54.8%, African 5.9%, Japanese 0.6%, Mixed 38.5%. Brazil's indigenous inhabitants number under 200,000.

Language	Portuguese	
Religion	Roman Catholic 89.1%, Protestant 6.6%, Atheist 1.5%, Spiritualist 0.8%, Afro-Brazilian 0.6%	

The Economy

GDP Total	1981 $284.7 billion.	
	Real rate of change:	
	Since 1980	− 3.5%
	1974-80 average.	+ 6.7%

GDP Per Capita	1981 US$2,333.26.	
	Real rate of change:	
	Since 1980	− 5.8%

Trade
Exports
1980 US$20.1 billion
1981 US$23.3 billion
Imports
1980 US$23.0 billion
1981 US$22.0 billion

Principal
Exports
(1980)
Manufactured goods 43.6%, processed raw materials 8.9%, soya products 10.9%, iron ore 7.5%, coffee 6.5%, sugar 2.5%.

Direct
Investment and
Re-investment
(1980)
USA 28.6%, West Germany 14%, Switzerland 10.1%, Japan 9.9%, UK 6.4%, France 4%, Canada 3.7%.
Total US$17.5 billion.

Major Trading
Partners (1980)
Exports to EEC 26.6%, USA 17.5%, Japan 6.1%, Argentina 5.4%, Middle East 5.2%.
Imports from Middle East 35.4%, USA 20.1%, EEC 16.7%, Argentina 13%, Japan 5%, Canada 4.3%.

Inflation
1980 110%
1981 95.2%

Minimum wage   1981 average in industrialized
               states:
               US$96.36 per month.

Foreign Debt   1973   12.6
(US$bn)   1974   17.2
               1975   21.2
               1976   26.0
               1977   32.0
               1978   43.5
               1979   49.9
               1980   53.8
               1981   61.4

Public Spending   Education   8.1%
(1978)   Health   2.2%
                  Military   14.0%

Literacy   1900   34.5%
                1940   43.6%
                1980   74.0%

Health   Life expectancy at birth 63.4 years (1975-80).
                Infant mortality per thousand live births 90-100
                (1977).

Sources: Instituto Brasileiro de Geografia e Estatistica, *Anuário Estatistico do Brasil 1981;* Estudos Apec, *A Economía Brasileira e suas Perspectivas,* Julho 1981; Central Bank of Brazil, *Annual Report,* February 1982; Inter-American Development Bank, *Economic and Social Progress in Latin America 1980 81.*

Chronology

1494   Treaty of Tordesilhas divided the world between Spain and Portugal.

1500   Portuguese explorer Pedro Alvares Cabral lands on Brazilian coast.

1502   King Manoel of Portugal licences Lisbon merchants to export brazilwood from the New World.

1530   First Portuguese colonization expedition under Martim Afonso de Souza.

1532   First sugar mills built in Brazil.

1549   Centralized government established.

1555-67	French colony in Rio de Janeiro.
1580-1640	Union of Spain and Portugal.
1624-54	Dutch colonize Bahia and parts of north-east Brazil.
1695	Gold discovered in Minas Gerais.
1727	Introduction of coffee into Brazil.
1763	Capital transferred from Bahia to Rio de Janeiro.
1808	Portuguese royal family leaves for Brazil during Peninsular Wars. João VI opens Brazilian ports to world trade and lifts restrictions on local manufacturing.
1810	Anglo-Brazilian treaties give Britain commercial dominance over Brazil.
1821	João VI returns to Portugal after Napoleon's defeat.
1822	Prince Pedro declares Brazil's independence and receives title of Emperor Pedro I.
1824	Brazil's first constitution promulgated. USA recognizes Brazil.
1825-8	War with Argentina over possession of Uruguay. Eventual agreement that Uruguay become an independent state.
1827	Britain consolidates commercial predominance through further treaty.
1844	First law to protect and stimulate local industry.
1858	Coffee becomes Brazil's principal export.
1865-70	Alliance with Argentina and Uruguay in war against Paraguay. Paraguay defeated.
1888	Abolition of slavery.
1889	The Emperor Pedro II dethroned and the republic established.
1890	Separation of church and state.
1891	New constitution promulgated.
1917	Brazil declares war on Germany.
1924-26	March of the revolutionary Prestes Column through the backlands.
1930	Getúlio Vargas comes to power.
1932	Uprising in São Paulo sparks off brief civil war.
1937	Vargas establishes authoritarian regime, the *Estado Nôvo*.
1942	Brazil declares war on the Axis powers (Germany/Italy/Japan).

4

1944	Brazilian Expeditionary Force sent to Europe, containing numerous young officers who were to take power 20 years later.
1945	Vargas regime deposed by the military.
1946	A new constitution promulgated.
1950	Vargas again elected president with populist support.
1954	Military threaten *coup;* Vargas commits suicide.
1960	Capital transferred inland from Rio de Janeiro to Brasília.
1961	The installation and resignation of President Jânio Quadros.
1964	Military overthrow President João Goulart with US assistance.
1968	Military hardliners crack down on political dissidents, intensify programme of censorship, repression and torture. Osasco strike crushed. Economic boom or 'miracle' begins.
1969	Kidnapping of US Ambassador Burke Elbrick. Military wages counter-guerrilla war. General Médici becomes president, initiating the harshest phase of the repression.
1974	Oil crisis puts an end to the 'miracle'. President Geisel takes power. Opposition makes enormous gains in senate elections.
1975	Journalist Vladimir Herzog dies under torture.
1977	'April package' drafted to contain opposition's potential electoral success. Geisel sacks hardline army minister Sylvio Frota.
1978	May — First strike in ten years.
	June — Progressive businessmen issue statement criticizing limited political reforms and calling for political and social changes including a return to democracy. Prior press censorship lifted.
	December — New National Security Act comes into effect; Institutional Acts abolished.
1979	March — General Figueiredo takes presidential office, promising to restore democracy.
	August — Amnesty bill becomes law.
	November — Two-party system scrapped.

1980   March — Government promises direct elections for state governors in 1982.

April-May — Military occupy ABC region of São Paulo to end massive metalworkers' strike. In Congress, national security charges brought against deputy João Cunha.

June — Bill to restore lost powers introduced in Congress.

August — Harsh immigration law pushed through Congress. Government appoints working party to draft new constitution.

September — Municipal elections postponed until 1982.

1981   June — PDS proposed electoral reform. Nilo Coelho, PDS Senate leader, says: 'These reforms are our instrument in the electoral battle. We must not lose power. We must win at any cost.' Main proposals include increasing the number of deputies from 420 to 500; lifting the legal obligation to vote; banning electoral alliances; limiting free time on television and radio and distributing it according to present electoral strength; extending the 'sublegenda' system (allowing winning candidate to collect votes from fellow candidates from the same party) to state governor elections. All these measures would boost PDS chances against the opposition.

August — *Conferência Nacional das Classes Trabalhadores* (Conclat) brings together 5000 worker delegates from all over Brazil, the most significant labour conference since the 1964 *coup*. Division apparent between militant *auténticos* led by Lula and backed by the PT, church, and other left-wing groups, and the conciliatory *Unidade Sindical* group comprised of *pelegos,* opportunist union leaders backed by the PCB, PC do B and PMDB. *Unidade Sindical* was formed in 1979 to respond to inroads made by the *auténticos* inside the unions. Both factions given equal representation on new commission to establish a centralized trade union movement, the *Central Única de Trabalho,* due for inauguration at the next Conclat.

October — São Paulo Governor Paulo Maluf orders state 'intervention' at Campinas University to thwart the university's attempts to reach internal democracy. Opposition wins major victory by rejecting the proposal to extend 'sublegendas' to elections for governors. The obligation to run one candidate per party is likely to split the PDS and assist opposition candidates.

November — Figueiredo announces electoral measures (the 'November package') to try to ensure that the PDS wins the 1982 elections. Voters can only back the candidates of a single party, parties must contest every single position in each locality where they have a branch or risk annulment of all votes, and parties must present candidates for the governorship of every state, ruling out coalitions or trade-offs between parties.

December — Opposition strikes back against 'November package'. PP dissolves and joins PMDB, which should allow PMDB to win around 16 of the 23 governorships. PT also gains; with the shift of the PMDB to the right, it becomes Brazil's third largest and principal socialist party. PT announces it will 'launch its own candidates at all levels'. PMDB accusations of PT splitting the opposition.

1982 January — Congress defies government by modifying *Lei das Ineligibilidades* to allow trade union officials dismissed by the government and anyone sentenced under the national security law to stand for election. This benefits Lula and other PT candidates, but PDS politicians have backed this movement in order to weaken the PMDB.

June — Government forces new political 'package' through Congress, threatening to expel any PDS member who fails to support it. Recognizing that the PDS has little electoral chance of success, the government hopes the new measures will ensure it holds power despite PDS losses. These measures include: blocking constitutional change by requiring a two-thirds majority; delaying municipal elections so as to extend the PDS mandate; reducing the size of federal deputies' constituencies so as to prevent wide support for any single candidate and reduce the chances of smaller parties; increasing the number of deputies from 420 to 477, by strengthening representation from rural states where PDS is strong; changing the electoral college to ensure PDS control.

July — Conclat II postponed until 1983. This decision opposed by the *auténticos* on the grounds that the building of a strong trade union movement ought not to take second place to the forthcoming elections.

November 15 — Elections for state governors, two-thirds

of the senate, the chamber of deputies, and the municipalities.

Political Parties

Prior to 1937

AL *Aliança Liberal* (Liberal Alliance). Pact formed for the 1930 election campaign led by Vargas and southern politicians.

PCB *Partido Comunista Brasileiro* (Brazilian Communist Party). Founded in 1922 as the *Partido Comunista do Brasil,* it was supportive of the Third International. After the collapse of the São Paulo uprising of 1924, Luís Carlos Prestes led the *tenentes* into the countryside to 'keep the revolution alive in the interior'. In 1935 it became committed to the peaceful road to socialism, organizing the *Aliança Nacional Libertadora* (ANL — National Liberation Alliance) as a popular front. By May of that year it was disbanded having posed a direct threat to Vargas. In November the militant wing of the party organized revolts in the garrisons of Natal and Recife. These risings were unco-ordinated and so easily crushed that Vargas was suspected of provocation. He declared a state of siege and imprisoned the left leadership. Prestes escaped but was recaptured in May 1936 and sentenced to 46 years in goal. In September 1937 the Army general staff 'discovered' a document outlining plans for a communist revolt. Known as the 'Cohen plan', this later proved to be fabricated by the *integralistas* as a pretext for a *coup.*

AID *Ação Integralista Brasileira* (Brazilian Integralist Action). Fascist party established by Plínio Salgado. Opposed Vargas in the 1937 election campaign, but influential in pushing his regime to the right when the *Estado Nôvo* was instituted.

PDP *Partido Democrático Paulista* (São Paulo Democratic Party). Allied with Vargas in 1930 election, but joined with PRP in the constitutionalist uprising in São Paulo in 1932.

PRP *Partido Republicano Paulista* (São Paulo Republican Party). Opposed Vargas in 1930. Joined with rival PDP in 1932.

In November 1937, Vargas abolished Congress and banned all political parties. This situation lasted until his overthrow in 1945.

1945 to 1964

PSD *Partido Social Democrático* (Social Democratic Party). One of the parties founded by Vargas after being ousted in 1945. It enjoyed the support of the rural oligarchy, and played a leading role in Congress and in government during this period.

PTB *Partido Trabalhista Brasileira* (Brazilian Labour Party). Established by Vargas in 1945 to organize the labour movement. Became a junior partner in alliance with the PSD. Amongst its leaders were the radical Leonel Brizola, governor of Rio Grande do Sul, and his brother-in-law, João Goulart, who was vice-president under Kubitschek and Quadros. Goulart became president in 1961, gradually edged by mounting popular pressure into adopting a radical reformist position, but unable to implement his project owing to the military takeover in 1964.

UDN *União Democrático Nacional* (National Democratic Union). Established in 1945 as a coalition of forces which opposed the pro-Vargas parties. The left intellectuals responsible for setting it up soon defected under pressure from the right-wing majority, comprised of local political bosses and the conservative industrialists and financiers. The UDN was generally disadvantaged in Congress owing to the PSD-PTB alliance, but managed to provide a slate for the successful presidential candidacy of the independent Jânio Quadros in 1961.

PCB *Partido Comunista Brasileira* (Brazilian Communist Party). Emerged again in April 1945 when Prestes was amnestied. It won 15 seats in the December congressional elections, and stood opposed to the Dutra regime. The onset of the Cold War and McCarthyism in the US was reflected in a purge of communists from the Brazilian civil service. In May 1947 the PCB was outlawed, but during the 1950s and 1960s it continued to work in the trade union movement. In July 1962 the communist-dominated CGT organized strikes in support of Goulart and campaigned strongly for its legislation. The PCB also carried out work among peasants in the north-east in competition with the church and the peasant leagues of Francisco Julião. Despite widescale mobilization of support for Goulart in March 1964, the PCB was quite unprepared for the ensuing *coup*.

1964 to 1979

During this period only two political parties operated legally.

ARENA *Aliança Nacional Renovadora* (National Renewal Alliance). Acted as the ruling party under the military dictatorship. Had strong links with the military and the ultra-conservative civilians implicated in the 1964 *coup*. Even within the military's own electoral rules, support for ARENA has consistently ebbed, and it remained in power only by constant changes of the rules in its favour.

MDB *Movimento Democrático Brasileiro* (Brazilian Democratic Movement). Acted as the official opposition under the military dictatorship. A number of its representatives in Congress were subject to the repression, and despite having a tame reputation, it attracted wide popular support consistently, in the absence of more authentic political opposition. As such, it became a vehicle for articulating liberal and reformist dissidence.

ALN *Ação Libertadora Nacional* (Action for National Liberation). Started in late 1967 as the Sao Paulo Communist Grouping led by Carlos Marighela, an ex-member of the PCB Executive Committee. When the PCB refused to send a delegate to the OLAS conference in Havana which raised the slogan of armed struggle, Marighela himself attended, broadcasting to Brazilians a call to arms over Havana radio. On his return he resigned from the PCB and other militants joined him in forming the ALN. In February 1968 they called for the launching of the armed struggle in urban areas, kidnapping the US ambassador in September 1969 and the Swiss ambassador in December 1970. Marighela himself was killed in a police ambush in November 1969; his successor, Câmara Ferreira, was killed in October 1970. It nevertheless remained one of the most active guerrilla groupings until its final defeat in 1972.

PC do B *Partido Comunista do Brasil* (Communist Party of Brazil). Formed in 1962 as the pro-Peking reflection of the Sino-Soviet split. It rejected Prestes' united front approach, and called for revolutionary organization of the peasantry. Influential in student circles. Breakaway groups worked with sugar cane workers in the north-east, or took up armed struggle only to be smashed by the police.

Armed political organizations during this period included:
COLINA *Comando da Libertação* (National Liberation Commando).
MNR *Movimento Nacionalista Revolucionário* (National Revolutionary Movement), responsible for setting up the Caparaó *foco*.
PCBR *Partido Comunista Brasileiro Revolucionário* (Brazilian Revolutionary Communist Party).

POC *Partido Operário Comunista* (Communist Workers' Party).
VAR-Palmares *Vanguarda Armada Revolucionário-Palmares* (Armed Revolutionary Vanguard — Palmares). Named after the seventeenth century slave republic of Palmares. Involved in rural guerrilla activity, as well as the kidnapping of the German and Swiss ambassadors, exchanged for 40 and 70 VPR prisoners respectively.
VPR *Vanguarda Popular Reaolucionária* (Revolutionary People's Vanguard).
Most of these organizations were smashed by 1972.

1979 to the present

PDS *Partido Democrático Social* (Democratic Social Party). Succeeded the rubber-stamp ARENA as the pro-government party, in order to give the political process some legitimacy under *abertura*. Holds slim majority in the Chamber of Deputies (223 out of 420 seats). Has strong party machinery and holds the edge over opposition in the rural areas where old-style political bosses still hold sway. Is the vehicle for what the government hopes will be the 'Mexicanization' of the political process, thus it is being groomed for a dominant role on a permanent basis in a nominally 'democratic' framework. Yet its monopoly of support cannot match the scale of the Mexican PRI, and it continues to lose ground, despite the electoral rules being skewed in its favour.

PMDB *Partido do Movimento Democrático Brasileiro* (MDB Party).Broad opposition party inheriting the mantle of the MDB. Represents the interests of Brazilian industrial capital and its allies of left and right. On the left it enjoys the support of the PCB and other groups which favour the notion of popular front. On the right, it has incorporated the *Partido Popular,* unable to go it alone under existing electoral rules. The PMDB stands to outdistance the PDS in the long run, despite the strictures of *abertura*.

PT *Partido dos Trabalhadores* (Workers' Party). Set up in the wake of the 1980 strikes by Lula and other labour leaders who recognize the need of more than just the union apparatus to deal with government repression. Membership grew rapidly in 1981, now standing at well over 300,000. Its strategy is to use elections to consolidate its structure and spread its ideas. Unlike other parties, the PT has regular meetings and party discussions. It is strongly rooted in the industrial workforce and in urban community organization, but is gaining ground in the rural areas with the active support of radicals in the church. Favours socialism, to be affected through mass democratic action. Factions are forming based on whether to increase or diminish the emphasis on an electoral strategy.

PTB *Partido Trabalhista Brasileira* (Brazilian Labour Party). The mantle of Vargas has been resurrected by his niece Ivete, but backing from ex-governor Leonel Brizola was short-lived. Brizola's exodus caused support for the PTB to fall dramatically.

PDT *Partido Democrático Trabalhista* (Democratic Labour Party). Brizola's breakaway from the PTB. Largely trading on Brizola's past populist record and political strength in Rio Grande do Sul. The party claims affinity with social democratic principles. In the long run its popularity will exceed that of the PTB but not of the PMDB.

PCB *Partido Comunista Brasileira* (Brazilian Communist Party). Resuscitated after Prestes' return when the amnesty was declared, it still remains illegal, and is campaigning for legalization. It supports the *Unidade Sindical* slate in the trade union movement, and the PMDB electorally, regarding the PT as mistaken for 'splitting' the opposition. Has played a conciliatory role in the labour movement, attempting to dissuade the leaders of the 1980 metalworkers' strike from persuing a confrontational strategy. Active in the national student union, where it holds key positions.

PC do B *Partido Comunista do Brasil* (Communist Party of Brazil). Also remains illegal. Controlled the leading opposition weekly, *Movimento,* until abandoning it in November 1981 to launch its own publication. Aligned with *Unidade Sindical* and has some support in the student movement.

Trade Unions

Brazil's labour code, the *Consolidação das Leis do Trabalho* (CLT) is closely modelled on Mussolini's *Carta del Lavoro,* and dates from its introduction in 1937. Trade unions are under the direct control of the labour ministry and subject to the regulation of the system of labour courts, *justiça trabalhista.* Their main source of income is the *imposto de contribuição,* a tax equivalent to one day's wages and automatically deducted by employers and paid directly to the state. This system has strengthened the role of the *pelegos,* trade union officials amenable to the state and to management. The word *pelego* means 'saddleskin', a metaphor indicating the smoothing of the rider's control over the horse.

During the democratic phase (1945-64), confederations of local unions were established for several sectors of industry. In general, these were affiliated to ORIT, the Latin American section of the International Confederation of Free Trade Unions, largely funded by the docile and collaborative labour movement of the United States. Yet Vargas's minister of labour, João Goulart, who went on to become vice-president, and later president, championed the cause of the labour movement. The influence of trade union leaders was extended and the *Comando Geral dos Trabalhadores* (General Workers' Executive) was set up in 1962 to circumvent the official organization controlling all unions, the *Confederação Nacional dos Trabalhadores da Indústria* (National Confederation of Industrial Workers). Yet the CGT was unable to develop an effective structure to withstand the repression which followed the military *coup* of 1964.

Despite the grave repression and persecution of workers under the dictatorship, and the imposition with renewed force of the CLT, workers patiently strived at shop floor level to rebuild a genuine democratic trade union structure. This took the form of constructing solid opposition to the imposed institutions. In the wake of the massive strikes in the metalworkers' unions around São Paulo, a number of *pelego* leaders began to be challenged by oppositionists known as *auténticos,* or genuine leaders, organised as the *Oposição Sindical* slate. In some cases they met with success, which caused the *pelegos* to strengthen their political control over the unions by drawing on a wider coalition of forces, including the PCB, the PC do B, and sections of the PMDB. They in turn were prompted to set up the *Unidade Sindical,* a front within the trade union movement to oppose the substantial gains made by the *auténicos,* many of whom played a prominent role in establishing the PT.

Both factions are keen to set up a unified autonomous trade union movement, the *Central Única de Trabalho* (CUT). In August 1981, the first National Working Class Conference (Conclat) met in São Paulo. One of its results was the setting up of a commission charged with the establishment of the CUT. The commission, in the interests of overall goals, was comprised of equal members of both factions. Yet divisions have persisted, not only as a reflection of the struggles within existing unions, but also because of the decision to postpone the second Conclat until after the november 1982 elections. This decision was supported by *Unidade Sindical* who justified it in terms of not diverting energies from the electoral process. However the *Oposição Sindical* have argued that any postponement plays into the hands of the government, and that primary consideration should be given to the goal of establishing the CUT rather than to elections.

The dictatorship has expressed its intention to dismantle the old labour code, and for this and other reasons, it is imperative that Brazilian workers organize themselves within a strong and centralized trade union apparatus. The struggles within the trade union movement will need to be waged in such a way that workers do not find themselves defenceless in relation to employers or the state.

2 The Vargas Years

Social Profile of Brazil

The rise to power of Getúlio Vargas in the 'Revolution of 1930' laid the ground for much of what has subsequently shaped the contemporary Brazilian state. Under Vargas began the shift away from the dominance of agriculture to that of the industrial sector of the economy. Yet Vargas failed to challenge the structure of landowning in which the few large landowners producing for the export market had the major share. To this day there has been no wide-ranging land reform, and this has enabled the large landowners to exercize power as a rural oligarchy (whereby the ruling group consists of a very limited number of people) in each of the Brazilian states, consistently obstructing social change.

Deriving their wealth mainly from coffee, the oligarchy controlled a large and impoverished rural workforce, and was able to squeeze out many of the *minifundistas,* or small property owners, who relied on the extended family for production. The small cultivators were often forced to sell their labour to the larger landowners during harvest time, becoming beholden to the latter as labour-tenants in many cases.

Producing for the world market linked the large landowners to the merchant class based in the cities, who ran the import-export trade. In some cases the capital accumulated through plantation farming and trade was ploughed into light industry — textiles and food processing — or, together with foreign interests, usually British, into investments in railways or power companies.

This sowed the seeds for the emergence of a class of industrialists. Less interested in producing for export and in liberal free trade policies, they began to look to the state to restrict imports of competitive foreign products (protectionism). In addition they began to attract workers away from the harsh exploitative conditions of the plantations. These factors set up contradictions between the industrialists and the large landowners, who still dominated the political process. It was therefore in the interests of the industrialists to back the forces around Vargas when they made their bid for state power.

With the growth of industry, sprang up a large industrial working class. Drawing on the strong anarchist and socialist traditions in Europe — much of the working class had originated from the waves of Italian and Iberian immigration in the late 19th century — workers attempted to consolidate their industrial strength. Much of Vargas's energies were devoted to the restriction and control of emerging working class power. Some of the controlling legislation drawn up in the 1930s still applies today.

Aside from the large landowners, the emerging groups of industrialists and the urban working class, other significant social forces emerged during the decade of the 1920s. Most dramatic of these was the movement of junior army officers or *tenentes* (lieutenants). Generally the sons of large landowners or urban professionals, the *tenentes* became politicized during a period of bitter rivalry between different sections of the ruling class over the presidential succession. Inevitably the army was drawn into the conflict, and junior officers staged an unsuccessful barracks revolt in July 1922. Eventually they were to link up with dissident civilian politicians in Rio Grande do Sul, São Paulo state and the north-east.

Rebellion grew, and the *tenentes* staged a protracted 'long march' through the Brazilian *sertão,* or backlands, between 1924 and 1927. Their political ideals included limited reforms; they advocated an end to the system of patronage whereby the large landowners became local political bosses, they favoured the introduction of the secret ballot to overcome corruption, and they promoted the idea of state assistance to rural workers living on the margins of consumer society. They hoped to base their armed rebellion on the support of workers and peasants. Although the 'long march' failed, the *tenentes* were influential in bringing Vargas to power and thus putting an end to the Old Republic founded in 1889.

The official armed forces had played a consistently important role in Brazilian politics. Strengthened by the state in order to wage the War of the Triple Alliance against Paraguay in 1867-70, the military played a part in the downfall of the Emperor and the installation of the Old Republic. Its role as 'moderating power' was even written into the constitution of 1891, enabling its intervention in politics if conflict occurred within the ruling civilian groups.

Other professional groups had also emerged as the state expanded its administrative apparatus, civil servants and teachers being important examples. Together with small business groups and shopkeepers, they formed part of a growing urban middle class, whose political interests were expressed more directly at a local than at a national level. Vargas was to take account of these groups in his construction of a supportive alliance, and won their backing for many of his populist initiatives.

The class differences in Brazil were further complicated by regional rivalries amongst the ruling oligarchies. This was usually expressed in the battle for the presidency, which had alternated between candidates from the economically important states of São Paulo and Minas Gerais. This had prevented other regional elites from exercising political power at the federal level, which intensified local resentment. Regionalism was a result of poor communications in Brazil, and had grown when the internal market for slaves — the only unifying national market — was abolished in the 1880s. The loose nature of the federation enabled state governments, particularly those of São Paulo and Rio Grande do Sul, to set up their own parliamentary forces. Mobilization of the latter helped Vargas to power.

Having examined the array of social forces in Brazil, let us turn to the circumstances which led to the 'Revolution of 1930'.

Threefold Crisis

The crisis which occurred at the end of the 1920s, enabling Vargas to take power, contained at least three major dimensions. In the economy, the gradual decline of the coffee trade was intensified by the international depression. Sparked off by the Wall Street Crash in 1929, the depression meant a severe cutback in the international demand for Brazil's coffee output. This had acute effects, because coffee was the country's principal export and had formed the basis for capital accumulation and industrialization in Brazil.

In addition, there was a profound political crisis, owing to the conflicts between different parts of the ruling class. Since the establishment of the Old Republic in 1889, the control of the federal government had remained in the hands of the São Paulo and Minas Gerais landed oligarchies, consisting of the rural political bosses, the self-styled *coroneís* (colonels) who ensured their political positions through a combination of patronage, coercion and vote rigging in the local areas under their control. Their position as coffee or cattle ranching tycoons had suffered during the depression. The relative

17

decline of the economic power and political leverage of this group made it vulnerable to a challenge on the part of an emergent opposition beginning to consolidate its power. This consisted of the new class of industrialists based mainly in the metropolitan areas of Rio de Janeiro and São Paulo, rebellious junior officers in the army (the *tenentes),* urban-based professionals, and the large landowners in those states (such as Rio Grande do Sul and the states in the north-east) formerly excluded from exercizing political power at the centre.

Thirdly, there was the appearance of a growing social crisis, as the emergent organized working class began to demand concrete social change. Largely excluded from political representation, workers were nevertheless emerging as a significant political force in Brazil.

Anarchists and Communists

Since the turn of the century, the Brazilian workers' movement had come under the influence of anarcho-syndicalism, then a powerful doctrine amongst workers in Southern Europe and the United States. It stood for non-hierarchical self-organization in general unions, and advocated the tactic of the general strike to overthrow the state and establish workers' control. Anarchists — many of whom had originated from Spain and Italy — were to be found at the forefront of huge workers' demonstrations, culminating in the wave of strikes in 1917 and 1920. Their ideas inspired many of the existing workers' organizations, including trade unions, mutual aid associations, sporting and cultural clubs, as well as worker-oriented newspapers and magazines.

Anarchist workers opposed the formation of alliances with other social classes in order to bring about change, and they were radically against workers participating in parliamentary politics. To them, the unions, besides being an instrument of direct struggle, also represented the embryo of the new egalitarian society which would be founded on the ashes of the capitalist state. Therefore they rejected the position of the communists, who advocated the need for a centrally-organized party of the working class, which would conquer power by stages. At first this meant operating in alliance with other sectors (particularly the emerging class of local industrialists), participating in elections and other institutions of the capitalist state. In a second stage, once the productive forces in Brazil had expanded, conflict between workers and capitalists would intensify, and only then would workers seek the overthrow of the capitalist state.

The two-stage theory meant that in the short term workers, in alliance with and led by local capitalists, were expected to favour a so-

1917: The Anarchist Strike in São Paulo

The massive rise in food prices during early 1917 triggered off substantial discontent in São Paulo. President Brás refused to see a delegation of workers, receiving backing from the minority leader in Congress. On 10 June, textile workers requested a 25 per cent wage rise, and when management refused, a strike was called. The strike soon spread, and the security forces were called out. Police broke up groups of pickets. The conflict intensified over the next few weeks, with strikers attacking police and strike breakers, provoked by the actions of the cavalry. Strike leaders were arrested and several workers were shot. The police chief's attempt to close the strike headquarters only strengthened the strike. By 12 July, there were 20,000 workers on strike. Troops continued to attack the resisting workers. Lighting, gas, public transport and mail deliveries came to a halt. The industrialists, increasingly perturbed, sought to negotiate once they had realized that repression was only hardening strikers' attitudes. Through the conciliation of the journalists, many of the demands of the strike committee were met: arrested strikers were released, wages raised by 20 per cent, the government agreed to respect freedom of assembly for trade unionists. It promised to end child labour, and nightwork for women and younger men. Price controls and health inspections were imposed on foodstuffs. The most significant strike in São Paulo before World War One, this paved the way for other strikes in Rio and elsewhere during the same year, and led to the implementation of the eight-hour working day by the state some months later.

called 'national democratic' revolution against the rural oligarchy, rather than a socialist revolution exclusively of their own making.

These points of divergence between the anarchists and communists were to have profound consequences for the workers' struggle in Brazil in the ensuing years.

In 1922 when the *Partido Comunista do Brasil* (PCB) was founded, the anarchist movement was somewhat disorganized due to a wave of repression unleashed by the authorities, in which the leaders of the strikes of 1917 and 1920 had been jailed and deported. The climate of repression — a recurring feature of Brazilian history — culminated in President Arturo Bernardes decreeing a state of siege, which suspended practically all the legal guarantees of civil rights until the end of his administration (1922-26).

In 1926, with the replacement of Bernardes in the presidency by Washington Luiz, and the ending of the state of siege, the workers' movement re-emerged. It was now under the influence of the communist party, and openly challenged the leadership of the surviving anarchists. The struggle between anarchists and communists was essentially over the control of the *sindicatos autónomos,* or independent unions, which had not been subordinated to the state, and of the other workers' organizations generally still under anarchist influence.

Alliance Making

To defeat their rivals, the communists fell back on a series of alliances with the traditional opposition, the liberal reformist groups which had struggled for power against the oligarchy. Thus, after the PCB was banned in 1927, the communists organized the *Bloco Operário e Camponês* (BOC — the Workers' and Peasants' Bloc), a legal political party which sought to attract trade unionists and rural workers, organizing committees throughout the country. By 1928 the BOC considered itself a national party.

Using the BOC, the communists sought to achieve parliamentary representation for the working class and nominated a worker, Minervino de Oliveira, as presidential candidate in the March 1930 elections. At the same time they sought to extend their political base through alliances with opposition groups to the left of the government. In line with this policy, they invited former army captain Luís Carlos Prestes to return from exile in Argentina and to join their ranks.

Prestes, who turned down the invitation, was the principal figure in the *tenentes* movement. Ultimately he joined the communist party in 1932 and became its secretary general, a position he continues to hold five decades later.

The growth of the BOC, which occurred at the same time as the creation of the *Confederação Geral do Trabalho* (CGT — the General Confederation of Labour) in 1929, was made possible due to the policy of class alliance pursued by the communists.

The traditional liberal opposition understood that in order to break the anarcho-syndicalist influence on the workers, it was necessary to strengthen the BOC. But this meant that the BOC was caught in a dilemma. In order to gain legitimacy amongst the working class, it had to be prepared to go so far as to challenge the law if necessary in pursuance of workers' interests. Yet at the same time it was restrained by the system of alliances which obliged it to remain within the constraints of legality.

In the play-off between legality and legitimacy, the BOC chose to operate within the existing laws. It was at this stage that the more traditional political groups acted to choke off the emerging political power of the workers and peasants. In October 1930, the *Aliança Liberal* (Liberal Alliance) of Getúlio Vargas and some of the *tenentes* took power by means of a *coup*. Representing a coalition of forces politically opposed to the sections of the oligarchy which had backed Washington Luiz, Vargas and his followers joined together to suppress the independent organization of workers. One of the key instruments of domination was to be the imposition of a revised trade union structure based on the corporatist model designed by Mussolini, Italy's fascist *duce*.

The 'Revolution of 1930'

On assuming power on 3 November 1930, Getúlio Vargas declared the Old Republic to be dead. His regime made room for new social forces, such as the industrialists eager to win state protection for locally manufactured goods which would replace imports. Yet essentially the same social classes remained in power, with certain regional realignments. Despite the reformist rhetoric which had attracted the *tenentes* to install Vargas in power, he was unable to challenge the land-owning oligarchy. Instead, one of his first moves was to rescue the coffee producers by offering state support for the financing of the ailing coffee trade. Even though Vargas came to rely on populist tactics, his style was authoritarian, and he moved rapidly to centralize power by removing the autonomy of the states. In addition all moves toward popular participation and independent working class organization were suppressed.

A decree of the newly created Ministry of Labour, dated 19 March 1931, revealed the regime's overall programme of disciplining the labour movement. It instituted a fascist-style corporate structure which continues to be in force today, severely restricting the process of free collective bargaining. In explaining its purpose, the decree stated that

the unions had to serve as buffers between the conflicting tendencies in capital's relations with labour.

Each occupational category of workers had to have a separate union, and each union was to become an instrument of collaboration between workers, management and the state.

In order to remove the old leadership of the unions, which, especially in São Paulo, consisted of European immigrants, the same law demanded that the number of Brazilian-born or naturalized workers had to be two-thirds of the total membership of each union.

21

Those bearing union office had, if they were naturalized, to have been resident in Brazil for over ten years, while for foreign nationals the period was thirty years. This decree therefore removed the majority of the most active class-conscious militants from the life of the unions.

In addition the Ministry of Labour was given sole powers to recognize the unions, and those that it chose not to recognize were outlawed. Once recognized, the unions would become subject to the permanent scrutiny of the Ministry's staff, who participated at meetings and conferences, controlled the accounts, and could penalize or dissolve the union executives if there was any 'disrespect' for the law.

This trade union structure which was perfected over the years, did not even owe its origins to internal union decision making; the state first cleared all its proposals on labour law with the bosses' organizations. In 1933, for example, Roberto Simonsen, the big business tycoon and founder of the São Paulo State Federation of Industries (FIESP), sent a document to Vargas in the name of FIESP fully endorsing the new labour legislation.

Big business also successfully obstructed the possibility of the government introducing social legislation until 1937. So in the first period of Vargas's rule the major task of the state was to restrict itself to the dismantling of the independent trade unionism of the past, replacing it with a corporate structure.

Estado Nôvo

Although initiated in 1931, the structure of corporatism — whereby the state gained full control of all industrial relations — was only fully implemented after 1937, with the setting up of the so-called *Estado Nôvo,* the 'New State'. This regime had come into being as a result of a military *coup* on November 10 which disrupted the normal transition of power to the succeeding presidential candidate and kept it in the hands of Getúlio Vargas. Vargas borrowed his new political style from the fascist dictatorships in Portugal and Italy, and cultivated the support of the local fascist movement known as the *Integralistas*. However, Vargas never formed a political party to back up the authoritarian phase of his rule. Instead, party politics diminished, congress was closed, and state governors became presidential appointees.

The principal objective of the *Estado Nôvo* was to set up a tight institutional framework for the domination of the working class, so that plans for the industrialization of Brazil might proceed without the unrest characteristic of the previous years. For example, the abortive

22

Civil War: Short-lived but Critical

On 9 July 1932 São Paulo staged an armed revolt against the Vargas government, hoping to broaden this into a civil war which would bring an end to the 'Revolution of 1930'. The political forces which combined against Vargas wanted Brazil restored to constitutional legality, opposed the role of the *tenentes* in government, and sought a share in state power which in 1930 had been lost to the politicians mainly from Rio Grande do Sul and Minas Gerais. Factories were converted to the production of armaments, middle class housewives donated their jewellery to finance the war effort, and their sons volunteered for the militia. However, the working class remained aloof and indifferent. The support expected from the anti-Vargas liberal constitutionalists in other states failed to materialize, and São Paulo was further isolated by its secessionist demands. The rebellion appeared as an expression of the discontent of the oligarchs, a point which Vargas was to play on ideologically. São Paulo was invaded by state and federal forces, and its capital encircled. When aerial bombing began, city businessmen appealed for a truce. The siege ended after two months, and the rebels surrendered to federal forces.

Vargas mollified his erstwhile opponents by conceding elections and a new federal constitution, which antagonized the *tenentes*. His magnanimity led to an easier acceptance of federal authority and enabled discipline in the armed forces to be restored. The ending of the rebellion enhanced Vargas's personal power, allowing him to neutralize the radical influence of the *tenentes*. Representatives from São Paulo were appointed to important posts in the government machinery.

rebellion in São Paulo in 1932, and the attempted communist insurrection of November 1935 in Rio de Janeiro and the north-east, indicated to Vargas that he could only consolidate his power by increasing the repression of the popular forces.

Fiscal and industrial policy-making powers were transferred from the states and placed in the hands of the federal government and its National Security Council. The harmonization of new banking, taxation and marketing policies helped in the setting up of a genuine national market. Although initially suspicious, the business community soon endorsed the *Estado Nôvo,* its consolidation of authority, its corporatist structure, its plan to help Brazil set up its own industries on the basis of domestic iron and steel production (based at Volta Redonda), and the nationalization of banks and essential industries.

The 1937 Constitution embodied many of these features, and

The Insurrections of 1935

In November 1935, the PCB under Luís Carlos Prestes deemed conditions ripe for a left-wing insurrection. Plans were prepared for a co-ordinated barracks uprising throughout Brazil. However, troops rose prematurely in Natal and Recife in the north-east, and were summarily crushed by loyal army units. The Popular Revolutionary Government in Natal fell, and Vargas declared a month-long state of siege. This precipitated the uprising in Rio, which Prestes hoped would spread rapidly so as to counteract the defeats in the north-east. By now Vargas had been alerted to these plans, and the uprising in Rio came as no surprise. The rebels were outnumbered and unable to broaden their initial gains. Defeat came quickly.

Vargas used the opportunity to arrest thousands of communists, anarchists, and supporters of the ANL front. Henceforth trade union leaders would have to hold 'certificates of ideological acceptibility', and these were not issued to communists. The fortunes of the PCB were set back for a decade.

regulated labour relations in a more interventionist way. The wages question is illustrative of the system: it proposed the creation of a minimum wage to cover the costs of the workers' basic needs. It could be greater than the legal minimum only if employers' organizations agreed on collective labour contracts with the respective unions. When no agreement was reached, the state was called in to arbitrate, appearing to play a neutral role, but generally acting in the overall interests of capital. Strikes were termed 'anti-social' and thus forbidden, leaving the workers with no legal powers against management. The *Estado Nôvo* declared that economic production was a function of the state, to be delegated to the representative corporations of capital and labour.

In effect the independent unions were crushed. Only the legally recognized unions could represent workers to the employer or the state. Unions were transformed into agencies which regulated the application of the labour laws to workers. Wages became determined by strict supply and demand criteria once free collective bargaining had been done away with, and at no time previously were employers provided with more favourable conditions for dominating the workers. This can be measured in real terms: taking 1914 as a base, the wages of qualified workers in the last year of the *Estado Nôvo, 1945,* had been reduced by 56 per cent.

Soon after the establishment of the *Estado Nôvo,* Vargas had

The Origins of Brazil's State-owned Steel Industry

For many years debate had proceeded around the setting up of a local large-scale steel industry in Brazil. Although the state, military, domestic and foreign interests recognized its necessity if Brazil were to become a successful industrial country, there was little agreement about who should finance and own the new steelworks.

An important candidate was the American industrialist, Percival Farquahar, who had gained contracts to mine iron ore in the Rio Doce valley in Minas Gerais. Although Farquahar was extremely influential, there was a great deal of opposition to him by other iron producers — Brazilian and foreign — as well as by exponents of nationalism amongst the military and politicians.

When Vargas came to power, the pressure of the nationalists, and particularly the *tenentes* in the army, for a fully state-owned steel industry grew. Brazil was endowed with adequate iron ore reserves as well as coal, and the domestic market for steel was increasing rapidly. By 1937 the army was determined to find a realistic alternative to the existing small-scale steelworks in order to establish the basis for a vigorous, self-sufficient national economy.

Yet external financing of the project was required. Vargas turned at first to private US steel companies. Du Pont, which had conducted a favourable survey of Brazil's steel prospects, showed little interest in investment. US Steel also sent a commission to Brazil. However, nationalist interests were unwilling to tolerate a large role for US Steel, and in January 1940 a new Mining Code appeared which excluded foreign ownership of subsoil resources or steel companies making use of local resources. The Code scared off US Steel, but the US State Department sought time to drum up support from other private US companies. When this failed, the State Department reluctantly agreed to furnish US$20 million through the Export-Import Bank to a Brazilian state-owned steel industry, in the absence of any private capital investment.

Part of the State Department's rationale was the war in Europe in which Germany was gaining the upper hand. Without US finance, Washington feared that Vargas would turn to Germany for support. It felt that the agreement 'assures for many years to come a close and useful co-operation between the two countries and set up an economic barrier against Germany'. Washington also foresaw a rising living standard for Brazil and an expanded market for US goods. Thus the support for the steel project, located at Volta Redonda after some debate, was one of the first conscious applications of an 'aid' strategy by the US directed at a developing country. For Brazil, it enabled the evolvement of an important state sector of the economy, and paved the way for its industrialization.

silenced all opposition and extinguished the *sindicatos autónomos,* the independent trade unions. Once the political power of the workers had been broken, it was then possible for Vargas to make paternalistic pronouncements about the necessity for class collaboration and denouncing the 'exoticism' of the notion of class struggle.

From 1940 rhetorical overtures were made to the workers, and as the World War intensified, the importance of their support in maintaining the economy's productivity became crucial. The war had cut trade with Europe, and the United States' market provided an alternative: rubber, coffee and iron were in great demand as Roosevelt re-armed. Brazil shifted away from the path which the *Integralistas* had mapped out; from a position of neutrality, Vargas edged the country into the war on the Allies' side, and went so far as to despatch three divisions to fight in Europe. The FEB, Brazil's expeditionary force, entered the fray under US tutelage, but acquitted itself bravely against the final Nazi offensive in Italy.

3 The Democratic Interlude

During the past half-century Brazilians have only experienced eighteen years of parliamentary democracy, between the removal of Getúlio Vargas in 1945 and the military *coup* of 1964. Even this system operated under rules which severely restricted the political options of the working class and ultimately cancelled many of the organizational and economic advances achieved in the course of the democratic interlude. The period also saw the gradual move towards economic expansion on the basis of foreign investment.

The Legacy of Vargas

The downfall of Vargas and the *Estado Nôvo* were not due to any popular uprising, but to several other factors. On the one hand the defeat of Nazism in Europe had some important repercussions. Not only was the authoritarian image of the *Estado Nôvo* discredited, but the regime's support inside the armed forces waned dramatically, as Brazilian soldiers fought the German troops in Italy. It became impossible for Vargas to continue to back those in his administration who supported Nazi Germany. For example, the head of Rio de Janiero's political police, Filinto Strubling Müller, notorious for repressing public anti-Nazi meetings, had to be dismissed.

On the other hand, there were repercussions from changes in the Brazilian economy. The war effort had led to further US involvement in mining and other strategic sectors of the economy. The war had also blocked the supply of foreign goods and stimulated the investment by large landowners in other sectors of the economy such as industry and finance. Brazilian society had become more complex, and Vargas's style of government less fit to administer this new variety of forces. In addition his somewhat nationalistic economic policies, which had been tolerated by the US in the context of the war effort, became unacceptable in peace time.

At the end of the war most anti-Vargas groups, ranging from the pro-US conservatives to the liberal anti-fascists, and including urban intellectuals as well as the more conservative anti-nationalist rural oligarchies, joined forces against the regime. 'Democratic' associations mushroomed, and the press overcame censorship and began to discuss the fate of the regime quite openly. The possibility of Vargas leaving office exacerbated the ideological split in the military, and this turned into bitter rivalry. Hoping to stay in power, Vargas attempted concessions: free elections, a new constitution and the release of political prisoners, who were mostly communist leaders and/or trade union militants.

But these concessions were too little and came too late. The same generals led by Pedro Aurélio Góes Monteiro who had helped Vargas to retain power in the 1937 *coup* which had set up the *Estado Nôvo*, now arranged for his peaceful removal from power.

Ingeniously Vargas, before his reluctant retirement, made the necessary arrangements for a later come-back by reorganizing his relatively loyal political base to suit the requirements of the new system. On the one hand he issued orders to provincial political bosses to re-group the local landed oligarchs into a conservative party, the *Partido Social Democrático* (PSD). On the other, he ordered the officials of the Ministry of Labour to organize the stooge *pelegos* — trade union officials — into a rival labour party, the *Partido Trabalhista Brasileira* (PTB). By tapping both these constituencies, and combining them against the forces who opposed him, Vargas left office in 1945 but retained formidable national support.

Most of the anti-Vargas forces joined together as the *União Democratica National* (UDN), which emerged as the second largest party after the PSD in the 1946 elections for a constituent assembly. The UDN soon lost its liberals and became a more genuine conservative party, representing the interests of the traditional export-oriented rural oligarchy (especially the coffee plantations), the newly developed banking sector linked to exports, and the conservative elements of the urban professional and small business groups.

For the whole period of parliamentary democracy which followed, the central electoral conflict took place between the UDN on the one hand and the uneasy alliance of the PSD and the PTB on the other. Numerically outweighed in congress for most of this time, the UDN rapidly developed an elitist ideology, establishing close links with the most reactionary sectors of the armed forces. Several abortive *coups* were staged by the military leaders closely connected to the UDN, until they finally succeeded in 1964.

The first test came in the 1946 elections for the constituent assembly, in which the Vargas candidate, General Eurico Gaspar Dutra, was elected president. The most unexpected development in these elections was the emergence of a fairly strong communist representation. Over half a million votes went to the communists. Although Dutra established a reputation of 'governing according to the little book' (the constitution), he did not hesitate to eliminate the communists from electoral politics. On the basis of a legal manipulation, the Supreme Court outlawed the communist party and stripped the elected communists of their seats in the assembly. The elimination of the communists from legal political life was the main achievement of Dutra's relatively uneventful administration.

Despite the election to the Assembly of several progressive politicians, the new constitution retained in full the corporative trade union structure of the *Estado Nôvo* period. The issue was never discussed by the Assembly, and even the communists failed to question the existing structure at the time.

The Return of Vargas

Vargas himself returned to presidential power in 1950 as the candidate of the incongruous PSD-PTB alliance. Initially there was a period of economic growth, which gave room for the campaign for the nationalization of the oil industry to succeed. As a result, under law 2,004 of 1953, Petrobras was set up as a state oil monopoly. Yet the economic problems of increased inflation and balance of payments deficit soon assumed the centre-stage. The trade unions held their first large strikes since the 1920s, and Vargas came down on the side of the labour-oriented PTB, which had replaced the opposition UDN as the second-largest party. The UDN politicians, alarmed at the strikes and the rise in nationalist sentiment within the armed forces, and spurred on by cold war ideology, encouraged the formation of the first right-wing paramilitary groups. These were to play an important role in the preparations for the 1964 *coup*.

In 1954, Army colonels issued a manifesto demanding the dismissal of Vargas's employment minister, João Goulart, opposing the new substantial increase in the minimum wage, and fulminating against government corruption. The signatories to the manifesto were later to appear as the main conspirators of 1964.

Military opposition to Vargas grew, particularly after an incident in

Petrobrás

Oil was discovered in Brazil in 1939, but until the 1950s production and proved reserves were insignificant. For Brazil, unlike elsewhere in Latin America, it was an entirely new industry. Instead of working out ways of adjusting to or compromising with foreign producers, Brazil was able to determine the shape of the industry in advance, whether by private, mixed or state control.

The army's role was decisive. After 1937 almost all state-sponsored industrialization in Brazil took place under military auspices. Oil was regarded by the military as a strategic commodity. The prime policy maker became General Horta Barbosa, director of the National Petroleum Council (CNP) under the *Estado Nôvo*. The legacy of his nationalist oil laws and policies lasted well after his resignation in 1943.

The immediate post-war period saw President Dutra's attempts to open the door to foreign participation, which invited attacks from nationalists within the military and Congress. With the post-war energy crisis, and the reluctance of foreign-owned utility companies to invest in overcoming the crisis, the oil debate became widespread and contentious. Nationalist pressure killed Dutra's proposed Petroleum Statute, and the slogan *o petróleo é nosso* (the oil is ours) was popularized.

By the time Vargas regained the presidency in 1951, on a progressive nationalist ticket, those who had advocated a state-owned monopoly had already won the arguments. In December of the same year Vargas sent a bill to Congress, which, after two years of debate, became Law 2,004 or 3 October 1953. This established a state-owned company called Petróleo Brasileiro SA. Known more widely as Petrobrás, it rapidly became Latin America's largest corporation and has maintained Brazil's oil resources and refining in the hands of the state.

which the palace guard attempted to assassinate a UDN politician. Air force and navy officers staged a rebellion demanding his downfall and a majority of the generals soon agreed to endorse this. In the face of such irresistable pressure, Vargas committed suicide. He left a *carta testimento,* a final open letter, dramatically denouncing the 'alliance between international and national groups' against the interests of the people.

Vargas's suicide in August 1954 produced a power vacuum which ended about a year later with the only *coup* in modern Brazilian history which upheld the constitution. This occurred when the Army minister, General Teixerira Lott, took to the streets with his tanks in order to assume the legal transfer of power to the newly elected president, Juscelino Kubitschek. The PSD-PTD alliance had won once again, with João Goulart as the vice-presidential candidate on the ticket.

The Assault of Foreign Capital

Kubitschek launched his administration in January 1956 ambitiously aiming at 'fifty years of development in five'. A former governor of Minas Gerais, he was the candidate of the PSD and represented the interests of the more conservative elements in the coalition of forces which Vargas had constructed. A believer in planned industrialization, he surrounded himself with technocrats who favoured private investment as a major component of the mixed economy. Brazil was opened up to unprecedented foreign penetration by transnational corporations, through offers of tax incentives, infrastructural facilities and easy profit remission. Economic growth averaged 7 per cent, reaching 10 per cent at the end of his term in office. Output increased dramatically: machinery by 125 per cent, electrical equipment by 300 per cent, and transport equipment by 600 per cent. Kubitschek encouraged the production of motor vehicles in Brazil by large US and European transnationals. This stimulated the construction of new highways crossing the country, and opened up the interior to greater capitalist penetration. To symbolize this, the capital was relocated to the purpose-built new city of Brasília, the construction of which was Kubitschek's most ambitious project.

In addition, regional development schemes were pioneered at this time and new authorities — such as SUDENE in the north east — were created, devoted entirely to the economic development of impoverished or remote parts of Brazil. However, much of this proved to be cosmetic, since Kubitschek, out of loyalty to his political base in the PSD oligarchy, failed to reform Brazil's anachronistic and unjust agrarian structure. At the same time he was careful not to antagonize his allies in the PTB, and refrained from stepping up repression of labour unrest.

Kubitschek's development strategy also went ahead with backing from some sections of the military who supported the idea of development in the context of strengthening national security. Lott, the general who had ensured his succession, became Minister of War in the administration, putting the military seal on its legitimacy. Kubitschek courted the armed services through increasing wages and providing them with more modern equipment. Thus the military appeared to benefit directly from the new phase of capital accumulation, and were further satisfied by Kubitschek's anti-communist pronouncements.

By the end of his term of office in January 1961, inflation had risen to almost 50 per cent per year. Part of this was due to massive state spending on the construction of Brasília and the road system, and part to the neglect of agriculture. Brazil's urban population rose by 60 per cent during the 1960s, reinforced by Kubitschek's policies, and yet little provision was made for the requisite expansion of food supplies, transportation, education, health, housing and social services.

The contradictions of his policy arose between the demands of the technocrats and foreign capital for a 'stabilization' policy to reduce inflation, and the growing demands of the popular movement for more social spending. To finance the massive deficit, the technocrats turned to the United States for a loan of US$300 million. The US would only agree to grant the loan on condition that Brazil submitted itself to an IMF stabilization plan. However the terms suggested by the IMF were severe, and Kubitschek refused the loan, fearing that an IMF-imposed austerity programme would jeopardize the projects on which his strategy had been based. Refusing the IMF terms alienated foreign capital, but gained the renewed support of the nationalists within the military and the popular movement.

Through indexing of wages to compensate for inflation, the living standard of many employees was maintained. However, the self-employed, and those on fixed wages, who constituted a large social stratum, had their incomes ravaged by inflation. It was in this atmosphere that an altogether new species of politician emerged to articulate their interests. A former mayor of São Paulo, Jânio Quadros, was elected governor of São Paulo state, defeating all the traditional political groups in a populist, anti-corruption campaign.

Exploiting the discontent and Quadros's success, the UDN offered him the prospect of being its presidential candidate. Meanwhile Kubitschek had failed to cement the PSD-PTB alliance. This meant that his replacement candidate, General Lott, the author of the constitutionalist *coup* in November 1955, was doomed to lose. His left-of-centre nationalist platform did not gain the support of most of the PSD.

The Outsider in Power

Quadros was thus elected by an unprecedented majority of votes. This expressed the populist response to glib promises of better, cleaner government. It was a landslide for those who had opposed the governing establishment. Curiously, João Goulart, from the opposing ticket, was again elected as vice-president.

The new president embarked on an austerity programme previously demanded by the International Monetary Fund, but rejected by his predecessor. Quadros nominated a conservative ministerial team, and, intoxicated by his personal political success, began to prepare the ground for a *coup* which would give him dictatorial powers. His lever was the popular sentiment against an obstructive congress, still dominated by the forces opposed to the 'stabilization' measures.

However the *coup* was naïvely conceived, and Quadros offered his resignation after seven months in office, hoping that in the ensuing crisis the military, key governors and perhaps the popular movement would act together to install him with full powers rather than allow for a takeover by Vice-President Goulart. Despite the shock this caused, the political parties within Congress which had consistently borne Quadros's humiliations, immediately accepted his resignation, and at the same time joined the military ministers in concocting a scheme to deny power to Goulart.

A succession crisis indeed followed, which was only resolved when Goulart's brother-in-law, Leonel Brizola, the PTB governor of Rio Grande do Sul, staged a popular rebellion with the assistance of some key army units, which forced the generals to compromise. Goulart, out of the country at the time, visiting China on an economic delegation, was permitted to return to assume the presidency, but the powers of his office were severely restricted. Once in office, Goulart was able to recover full powers by means of a national referendum.

The Birth of the Conspiracy

Initially, Goulart entered office rather cautiously. However, his period of administration was marked by the unleashing of popular forces and aspirations. The conservative forces came under threat, since their previous domination began seriously to be checked by successive electoral victories of the politicians and political groups representing the masses. The political conflict thus sharpened.

New forms of popular and worker organization emerged at this stage. In the north-east, Francisco Julião created the Peasants' League movement, demanding better working conditions in the countryside and a thorough agrarian reform. In Pernambuco large landowners were restrained from repressive action by the governor, Miguel Arraes, who had been elected by an alliance of popular parties. This had occurred despite the efforts of the US-based transnational corporations to finance a powerful combination of conservative groups with large sums of money.

The Birth of the Peasants' League

In itself Galiléia has little significance, being a former sugar plantation composed of undernourished, sloping, rocky soil. There are one hundred and forty families living on its five hundred hectares, most of them extremely poor, living off plots of one or two hectares. Here I began my first propaganda campaign to peasants united in a League. A fair number of them had ballot rights which ensured them some immunity against the local political bosses. The owner was absentee, and only went to Galiléia at the year's end to collect rents; so the menacing presence of the League on his land was reported by neighbouring *latifundio*-owners.

There then began a legal battle after the peasants were given notice to quit *en masse* in six months; but a legal certificate of leasehold existed which gave me a chance of keeping the case open for several years. But I went further and focused attention on the Galiléia case, not only among the peasants who had come long distances to join in meetings, but also among all the poorer classes; and as soon as the dispute became official and local, as well as southern journalists started reporting the affair, the cause gained momentum. The landowners' reaction was to turn the Galiléia affair into a police case; but they failed and I managed to turn it into a civil case. The conservative press didn't take long to realize that this was the germ of a movement capable of arousing the nation in favour of agrarian reform without violent social upheaval — i.e. a superficial agrarian reform when the sacred principle of private property might escape unscathed. If the land were expropriated for cash compensation and then sold to the peasants at its 'real' value (and not its original value or at the value declared for tax purposes . . .) then everything would be 'humane', 'legal' and 'Christian'. By this simple device money would find its way into the *latifundiários'* pockets from public funds extorted from the people for exhausted or under-exploited land; and the League, by collaborating in the ruse, would soon enjoy the unanimous applause of the most reactionary classes in the country, the landowners.

We had to oppose a move which would convert the League into a weapon turned neatly against the peasants themselves, though it wasn't easy, especially when one considers the natural desire of the peasant to get freehold of his holding at any price, since possession means liberation. Galiléia showed the region's peasantry the truth that agrarian reform doesn't simply mean expropriation but the devolution of the land to the people who work it without any other condition save that they should simply continue to cultivate it. By much writing and talking on the subject I managed to convince the majority of peasants in principle that they should not be fooled by promises of land to be had at ridiculous prices plus interest on

➤

instalments, *plus* conditions preventing them from disposing of the land at liberty, since a series of restrictions and obligations would be included which would incur loss of the land if they were not observed. On top of this they had to work the land! One might as well be a tenant for life as be an owner for a day. Thanks to this question of expropriation we managed to suspend rent payments at Galiléia for four years; and then, when the land became the property of the Land-Settlement Company,* we kept the legal case going another four years until another progressive-minded attorney sympathetic to the popular cause simply handed over the land to its original tenants.

Galiléia thus became famous throughout Brazil as an example of an agrarian reform in embryo; and from its steep, rocky soil and its peasants, united in the first League truly founded by themselves, we struck the spark which spread the movement throughout the North-East. With it we awoke thousands of peasants to political consciousness. Reports and articles published on the Galiléia affair and its impact on the region would fill a thick volume. Fierce debates sprang up during the whole long course of the tenants' struggle for the right to settle on the land they had been renting; and for the reactionaries it was a dangerous precedent harmful to social peace since left-wing extremists might use it to win support among rural workers and so expand this initial movement into something hundreds, thousands of times greater, so turning the North-East into one enormous, uncontrollable Galiléia.

*A state organisation for administering and redistributing land in areas of social tension.

Francisco Julião, *Cambão — The Yoke: The Hidden Face of Brazil,* Penguin, 1972, pp.125-127.

At the same time, the first ever national meeting of peasants took place in Belo Horizonte, putting forward the slogan *'reforma agrária na lei ou na marra'* (land reform by law or by force). Sectors of the Catholic-oriented *Ação Popular* (Popular Action) claimed adherence to Marxist ideas, and were active within the *União Nacional dos Estudantes,* the national students' union.

In the south, Leonel Brizola radically challenged foreign interests by taking over a large US-owned utility company in his state, a subsidiary of International Telephone & Telegraph (ITT).

In the large urban areas, trade unionists began to articulate their demands more firmly. They sealed a joint-action pact between the main unions, known as the *Pacto de Unidade e Ação* (PUA), and this led to the launching of a massive campaign to form a central union body, the CGT. With unprecedented confidence and strength, a series of strikes succeeded one after another.

Urban and rural forces combined under the banner of *reformas do base* (grassroots reforms), a series of structural changes including the enfranchisement of illiterates and soldiers, and a serious land reform. The land reform proposals were taken up by Goulart's planning minister Celso Furtado in his *Plano Trienal* (three-year plan), and Goulart hesitantly began to hitch his political bandwagon to the seemingly irrepressible popular movement.

Goulart's populism and nationalism operated largely on the level of rhetoric, and he was constrained by the conservative majority in congress and by the crisis in the Brazilian economy. By 1963, the rate of growth of the economy slowed down to 1.5 per cent, and inflation leapt to 80 per cent. The right, unable to offer alternatives to the popular demands, began to conspire for the downfall of the government, especially after Goulart's powers were restored through a referendum. Conspiracies were initiated amongst the military, landowners' associations, bankers and conservative press barons. The offices of the newspaper *O Estado de S. Paulo* served as the headquarters for one of the conspiratorial groups.

Both Goulart by his hesitancy, and the popular forces through placing too much faith in the 'national bourgeoisie' (local capitalists who derived benefits from nationalist and populist programmes) badly misread the situation. In fact, since the days of Kubitschek, the national bourgeoisie had been linked with foreign interests, and had already joined the conspiracy. The feared impact of the Cuban revolution on the rest of the continent had made most capitalists receptive to the anti-communist propaganda of the official church and the US State Department. Yet the popular forces were insufficiently organized to challenge the state, and although they sought political reform and economic redistribution, were not in a position to constitute a real threat to the maintenance of Brazil's market economy.

In response to a rebellion by solders and marines (later discovered to be the work of *agents provocateurs*) Goulart staged an impressive mass rally in Rio, which he used to announce the introduction of some of the *reformas do base*. The rally and Goulart's indecisive handling of a sailors' mutiny in Rio antagonized the civilian and military forces who opposed reform, and provided catalysts for the consolidation of an armed assault on the regime. Within days the military *coup* was organized. It faced little resistance, and there was no bloodbath.

Goulart fled into exile, thousands of arrests were made throughout the country, and the popular movement was severely curbed. The generals installed political and cultural terror in the name of saving Brazil from 'communism'. The brief democratic interlude was over.

4 The Dictatorship Consolidates

Analysis of the New Regime

The economic aims of the various groups that supported the *coup* were both well defined and mutually compatible. Mainly they involved creating the climate for investment, particularly from abroad, by reducing the inflation rate, and lowering real wages. The privileges of the rural oligarchy had also to be protected.

The basic economic strategy of the new regime was drawn up by Roberto Campos, the planning minister, in the so-called 'government plan for economic action' which covered the period 1964-66. Campos had prepared the ground carefully before the *coup,* using his position as a partner in a consultancy firm called Consultec, which also included other high-ranking government officials among its directors. As Goulart's ambassador to Washington, he had also broadened his connections with US business.

But when it came to the political means whereby the economic strategy was to be implemented, or the political model to be adopted by the regime, serious differences of opinion soon became apparent among the conspirators. One stumbling block was the widespread ambitions for the presidency among leading politicians who supported the *coup,* another was the historically deep divisions among the armed forces.

Consequently it took ten years for the nature of the regime to become clearly established — the first five years saw the marginalization and eventual subordination of the civilian politicians who had supported the *coup;* the second five years was taken up with 'refining' the system. By the end of that time, however, a form of

With a Little Help from Their Friends

The US government, labour bureaucrats and corporations also moved in to bolster the new regime, through the American Institute for Free Labour Development (AIFLD). Brazilian trade union leaders were already being trained by AIFLD in Brazil and the United States before the military takeover. The AIFLD ideology of 'business unionism' — the harmony of interests between labour and capital, combined with the rabid anti-communism — would serve as a useful tool in reorganizing the Brazilian labour movement in the post-*coup* mould.

In 1963, the *Instituto Cultural do Trabalho* (Cultural Institute of Labour), AIFLD's organizational base in Brazil, sent 33 influential trade union leaders to the United States for a three-month course. Upon returning to Brazil, the majority joined the conspiracies that ultimately toppled the populist government of Goulart. In a 1965 *Nation* interview, William C Doherty, AIFLD's Executive Director, stated that 'the crop of Brazilian graduates of the AIFLD course that came back to their country in 1964 were composed of elements so active that they became intimately involved in some of the clandestine activities of the revolution (the military's terminology for their dictatorship) before it occurred. Many of the trade union leaders, some of whom were effectively trained in our institute, were involved in the defeat of Goulart.'

Three months after the *coup* and government interventions in more than 450 unions, Doherty commented to the Brazilian press 'that the Brazilian trade unions are enjoying a freedom never seen under Goulart'.

Since the military coup, AIFLD 'educational ' programmes have trained over 50,000 Brazilian trade unionists in their in-country programmes, and sent over 400 to the Front Royal Institute in Virginia for advanced course work. This layer of union bureaucrats form the core of the *pelegos* in the Brazilian trade union structure.

Jim Green, 'Liberalization on Trial: The Workers' Movement', *NACLA Report on the Americas,* 13,3 (May-June 1979), pp.17-18.

dictatorship unique in many respects had emerged. Its principal characteristics are as follows:

● a highly centralized federal government controlled by the military, dominating weak state governments with little or no military participation;

● the widespread appointment of retired military officers to influential and often leading roles in the state machinery and state companies;

● rotation of the presidency every five years, a process usually preceded by a crisis of succession as different groups within the armed forces struggle for power. In this 'dictatorship without a dictator', only four-star army generals are eligible to become president;

● a large and lavishly paid civilian technocracy, the 'expert' section of the bureaucracy, particularly well entrenched in economic policy-making, an area in which the military have virtually no say;

● the dominance of business interests over most other interests;

● the maintenance of some of the usual political institutions, in particular a functioning congress and regular elections, to provide the regime with some basis for legitimacy;

● frequent changes in the rules of the political game, and periodic purging of potential leaders thrown up by popular movements or the popular vote, so as to maintain control of the political process.

The first great purge took place immediately after the *coup,* when 100 leading politicians and trade unionists, members of the armed forces opposed to the *coup,* congressmen, state governors and intellectuals were stripped of their political rights for ten years — those with an elected mandate lost it. Widespread dismissals, arrests and expulsions took place in the local, state and federal administrations, in the universities and armed forces. Up to 1977, it is estimated, the regime annulled the political rights of 4,682 citizens, including 1,261 military men, 300 university teachers, 50 state governors or mayors, three former presidents (João Goulart, Jânio Quadros and Juscelino Kubitschek), diplomats, federal deputies, judges (not exempting the Supreme Court), journalists, union leaders, public servants and ordinary workers.

What remained of congress duly rubber-stamped the military's choice of General Humberto de Alencar Castello Branco as the regime's first president. Castello Branco was a leading representative of the 'sorbonnist' faction of the armed forces, which gained its name from a short period of French influence within the *Escola Superior de Guerra,* the Higher War College, which had been set up in 1949. The intellectually-inclined 'sorbonnists' took a close interest in politics and were fiercely opposed to nationalist and left-wing positions.

Torture and assassination were not part of the stock-in-trade of the regime in its early days, although several cases occurred, particularly in the north-east and in Goiás. Soldiers with known links to popular movements were tortured in army barracks.

The main opponents of the 'sorbonnists' within the army were the so-called hard-liners *(linha dura)*. Hard-liners are for the most part ordinary soldiers, strongly anti-communist, inflexible, anything but intellectual, strongly nationalistic, and much less enthusiastic about foreign capital than the 'sorbonnists'. Some hard-liners are as fanatically nationalistic as they are anti-communist.

The first real test for the 'sorbonnists' came in October 1965 when, despite the purge of the political opposition, it won the elections for state governors in several states, including two of the most important, Rio de Janeiro and Minas Gerais. Hard-line colonels sent an ultimatum to Castello Branco via the anti-'sorbonnist' army minister, General Artur Costa e Silva, demanding immediate action to rectify the situation. This paved the way for the first of what proved to be a series of so-called institutional acts, decrees conferring special powers on the president and in many cases overriding constitutional rights. Among other things, they gave the president the power to strip any citizen of his or her rights for up to ten years, to revoke any elected mandate, and to disband any political party. They also made elections for the presidency and state governorships indirect, subject to votes in Congress rather than universal suffrage.

In 1967 a new constitution was introduced by Costa e Silva, who had become the natural successor to Castello Branco. It strengthened the powers of the president and reduced those of Congress, which lost its right to legislate on economic matters. Moreover, the existing political parties were abolished and replaced by a two-party system, comprising the pro-government *Aliança Renovadora Nacional* (ARENA) and the opposition *Movimento Democrático Brasileiro* (MDB). A new national security law was also introduced which severely curtailed political rights.

Shop-floor Resistance is Suppressed

It was the working class which suffered most under the government's economic policy. In 1967 job security was abolished, and three-and-a-half years after the *coup* had taken place, the real value of urban workers' wages had fallen by 35-40 per cent. In 1968 an upsurge of shop-floor militancy posed a serious threat to the regime.

In Contagem, an industrial suburb of Belo Horizonte, 15,000 metalworkers from 19 firms came out on strike demanding the restoration of job security and a 25 per cent wage increase. The military were rather taken by surprise by the movement, and after long negotiations acceded to some of the workers' demands. Three months later, however, when a similar movement broke out in

Taming Party Politics

Having added some very authoritarian measures to the Brazilian constitution by way of Institutional Act No.2, Castello Branco next attempted to endow the civilian political process with a 'normal' face. He proved his 'sorbonnist' credentials by dissolving extreme right-wing groupings and agreed to the functioning of a tame congress. Congress would be useful in legitimating the army's nominees to high executive office. So instead of dismissing the powers of the parliamentary deputies, Castello Branco announced Supplementary Act No.4 on 20 November 1965, with procedures for setting up new political groupings to replace the dissolved parties.

The catch was that new parties could only be constituted if they commanded a minimum of 120 deputies and 20 senators. Since there were 409 deputies and 66 senators in total, it was impossible to form more than three new parties. In practice, this number was reduced to two when 250 deputies and 40 senators indicated that they would support the government. They took the name of ARENA, *Aliança Renovadora Nacional* (National Renewal Alliance) and expressed personal loyalty to Castello Branco.

The opposition had no choice but to unite within a single organization, which took the name *Movimento Democrático Brasileiro* (Brazilian Democratic Movement), MDB. Even so, it was two senators short of the minimum required. The *Jornal do Brasil* observed that 'in order to make the two-party formula become a *de facto* reality, the government was almost obliged to *lend* two senators to the opposition party'.

Although the men were the same, the realignment was as follows:

	Deputies	Senators	Source
To ARENA	83	16	UDN
	67	15	PSD
	38	4	PTB
	34	—	Others
To MDB	73	13	PTB
	40	5	PSD
	6	1	UDN
	6	—	Others

Osasco, on the outskirts of São Paulo, the authorities adopted very different tactics. This time 3,000 workers occupied their factories to back their demands, but the strike was violently crushed with the use of soldiers. During the following ten years working class activities were stifled.

The wave of working class militancy was followed by student unrest, a series of bombings carried out by an *agent provocateur* believed to be linked to hard-liners in the army, and the first actions of urban guerrilla groups. Using an anti-military speech in Congress by federal deputy Márco Moreira Alves as a pretext. Costa e Silva closed down Congress in December 1968 and issued Institutional Act No.5 (AI-5), which suspended the right of habeas corpus for political detainees. The long night of terror had begun.

Institutional Act No.5 has been widely called the '*coup* within the *coup*', representing as it did the victory of the hard-liners' policy of violent repression over more conciliatory approaches to solving the nation's problems. By closing the usual channels of protest and demand, the act did much to encourage the left to answer the regime's violence in its own terms. Armed resistance however proved largely unsuccessful and resulted in the elimination of almost an entire generation of radical leaders. In the period that followed, some 78

Institutional Act No.5

The justifying paragraphs of the Act read very much like those of April 1964, and October 1965 (Institutional Acts Nos.1 and 2), with emphasis on 'guaranteeing the authentic democratic order, based on liberty, respect for human dignity, combating subversion . . . and the fight against corruption'. Draconian as its provisions were, the populace was reassured that they would be employed only to 'confront directly and immediately the problems of restoring internal order and the international prestige of our country'. The Act granted the president authority to recess legislative bodies, to intervene in the states without limit, to cancel elective mandates and suspend political rights, to suspend constitutional guarantees with regard to civil service tenure, etc., to confiscate property acquired by illicit means, issue complementary acts, and to set aside the right of habeas corpus. All such actions were to be beyond judicial review. Complementary Act No. 38, issued at the same time, closed Congress indefinitely. Thus the 'humanization' of the revolution promised by Costa e Silva two years earlier ended with the imposition of censorship stronger even than that known during the *Estado Nôvo*. As the hard line had exploited a political crisis to radicalize military opinion and force Castello to the right in 1965, now it manoeuvred Costa into a position in which he had to yield to their demands.

Ronald Schneider *The Political System of Brazil*, Columbia University Press, New York, 1971.

---

political activists disappeared, 178 were killed in clashes with the police or while under arrest, and another 45 went missing, presumed dead, following an attempt by the Maoist party to establish a rural guerrilla base in the Amazon.

Another important effect of the guerrilla movement was that it led to the formation of a group of torturers, including members of all three armed forces and the police. Some of those involved, whether as torturers or protectors, now hold high positions. They include four-star generals such as Antônio Sandiera, Mílton Tavares and Ernani Ayrosa.

Marighela and the Guerrilla Movement

The roots of the guerrilla movement run back to 1962, when a group espousing Maoist ideas of revolution initiated in the countryside, broke from the PCB, though without attempting at the time to put their ideas of armed struggle into practice. In 1966 left-wing soldiers and sailors, with some encouragement from former state governor Leonel Brizola, made an unsuccessful attempt to establish a guerrilla base in Caparaó, not far from Rio de Janeiro.

But the decisive breakthrough for the movement followed the participation of a delegation from the PCB in the Latin American Solidarity Organisaton (OLAS) conference in Havana in 1967. On returning from the conference, Carlos Marighela, the PCB leader in São Paulo, with the support of many party members, particularly intellectuals and middle class students, launched the manifesto known as *Ação Libertadora Nacional* (Action for National Liberation), which called for the transformation of the political crisis into a popular armed struggle against the military regime. Marighela and his followers were immediately expelled from the PCB, which wanted nothing to do with armed struggle. Marighela's break with the PCB was symptomatic of the disillusionment felt by many on the left at the party's obvious inability to mobilize against the regime. In his Guevara-inspired manifesto, Marighela stressed that

Our main activity is not building a political party, but unleashing revolutionary activity . . . guerrilla activity is in itself the command of the revolution . . . the revolutionary's duty is to make revolution.

As the opportunities for lawful political activity were systematically snuffed out, Marighela's alternative seemed all too logical to many on the left. Almost every political group gave birth to at least one faction committed to armed struggle..

The leading guerrilla groups were Marighela's *Ação Libertadora*

Nacional (ALN), *Vanguarda Popular Revolucionária* (VFR), at one time led by army captain Carlos Lamarca, and *Movimento Revolucionário 8 de Outubro* (MR-8), another split from the PCB, and which was responsible for the spectacular kidnapping of the US ambassador, Burke Elbrick, in September 1969.

However logical Marighela's call to arms had seemed to certain revolutionaries, in practice the guerrillas were politically ineffective and very short-lived. After a small number of spectacular actions, most groups found themselves devoting most of their time and energies to simple survival. No mass movement of resistance to the regime emerged, as the guerrillas had expected. Nor was there any important political reservoir from which they could draw support and reinforcements.

Torture Rules

Torture is the traditional weapon of the Brazilian police for extracting information and confessions. It had also been used for political purposes during the *Estado Nôvo* and in the 1950s when the struggle between nationalists and the supporters of foreign capital was at its height. Now it was only natural that the security forces should resort to the same methods to crush the guerrillas. Yet the brutal and systematic way in which it was used on hundreds of detainees was unprecedented in scale and severity.

For the security forces it was a matter of catching individuals or small groups. The most efficient way to do this was simply by tearing out the information by the crudest use of violence. The torture began immediately a suspect had been arrested, often in the vehicle in which they were being taken to the police headquarters, in order to get the information leading to the next link in the chain before 'the enemy' suspected something was wrong. The suspension of habeas corpus for political detainees, and the censorship of the media, played an important part in providing the security forces with the free hand they wanted.

Horrendous methods of torture were used. Many prisoners were killed, including well-known left-wing leaders such as Mário Alves and Joaquim Câmara Ferreira. Marighela himself died in unclarified circumstances in an ambush laid by the notorious head of the police death squad in São Paulo, Sérgio Fleury. Fleury's death squad combined the cold-blooded assassination of petty criminals with the hunt for guerrillas.

In addition to the DEOPS political police, and the specialised intelligence units of each service, CIEX (army), CENIMAR (navy)

Testimony of a Torture Victim

In May 1970, Marcos Arruda was arrested in São Paulo and held in the offices of Operação Bandeirantes, a section of the security forces who systematically used torture. He was released by February 1971.

They ordered me to strip completely: I obeyed. They made me sit down on the ground and tied my hands with a thick rope. One of the six or seven policemen present put his foot on the rope in order to tighten it as much as possible. I lost all feeling in my hands. They put my knees up to my elbows so that my bound hands were on a level with my ankles. They then placed an iron bar about eight centimetres wide between my knees and elbows and suspended me by resting the two ends of the iron bar on a wooden stand so that the top part of my body and my head were on one side and my buttocks and legs on the other, about three feet from the floor. After punching me and clubbing me, they placed a wire on the little toe of my left foot and placed the other end between my testicles and my leg. The wires were attached to a camp telephone so that the current increased or decreased according to the speed at which the handle was turned. They began to give me electric shocks using this equipment and continued to beat me brutally both with their hands and with a *palmatoria* — a plaque full of holes — which left a completely black hematome, large in size than an outstretched palm, on one of my buttocks. The electric shocks and the beatings continued for several hours. I had arrived at about 14.30 and it was beginning to get dark when I practically lost consciousness. Each time I fainted, they threw water over me to increase my sensitivity to the electric shocks. They then took the wire from my testicles and began to apply it to my face and head, giving me terrible shocks on my face, in my ears, eyes, mouth and nostrils. One of the policement remarked 'Look, he is letting off sparks. Put it in his car now'. The group of torturers were under the command of Captain Albernaz and consisted of about six men, amongst them Sergeants Tomas, Mauricio, Chico and Paulinho.

Extracted from Amnesty International, *Report on Allegations of Torture in Brazil,* London, 1972.

and CISA (air force), special joint units were also set up to track down the guerrillas. The most prominent was *Operação Bandeirantes* (or Oban) set up in São Paulo in July 1969, and which involved both military and police personnel. The success of Oban, with its three teams working around the clock, led to the establishment of similar units in Rio de Janeiro and Brasília. For several years these units existed only unofficially — no mention of them was to be found in any armed services list. Later they were formalised under the name of DOI-CODI — *Destacamento de Operações Integradas* — *Comando de Defesa Interna* (Detachment of Integrated Operations — Internal Defence Command).

Various companies and businessmen gave financial and technical aid to the torturers, either because pressure was put on them or because they actively wished to do so. A prominent example of the latter was Pery Igel, chairman of an important petrochemical company who took a personal delight in attending torture sessions. He was later killed by a guerrilla commando.

With ample funding and a complete lack of accountability, the DOI-CODI groups became the heart of what was known as the 'industry of repression'. Once their purpose had been served, however, they became a liability for those sectors of the regime which considered that the time was approaching for easing off the rigid restrictions on the nation's political life. Fearful that such a move might lead to their being investigated and brought to trial for what were, after all, illegal activities, the torturers came to constitute an important hard-line pressure group fiercely opposed to liberalization.

But the effects of their actions were felt elsewhere. The armed forces themselves were deeply compromised, not only by their tacit acceptance of the service provided by the torturers, but also in their subsequent efforts to maintain the cover-up. Whatever was done in later years to curtail DOI-CODI's activities, and whatever the strength of their commitment to more open policies, Presidents Geisel and Figueiredo both made it clear that no 'muck-raking' of the past would be tolerated. In this way the armed forces as a whole have taken on some of the responsibility for torture.

Moreover, once their job had been done and the guerrillas eliminated, the torturers did not simply disappear or return to their former functions. Having lost their *raison d'être,* they set out to create another one. The kidnapping and assassination of 25 left-wing activists in 1974-75 had little to do with safeguarding the state against its enemies, and much to do with guaranteeing the torturers' security and jobs.

The Mechanics of the 'Miracle'

The boom known as the Brazilian 'economic miracle' started in 1968, well before the urban guerrilla movement took off. Following the defeat of the workers at Osasco, the wage squeeze policy already in force could be applied more rigorously, while the government's monetary and fiscal policies worked, as intended, to put many small or inefficient firms (the vast majority of them Brazilian-owned out of business.)

Central to the success of the boom was the reduction in the real value of the minimum wage, which was what some 25 per cent of rural workers and 45 per cent of urban workers received. Between 1963 and 1973 the real value of the minimum wage fell by about 25 per cent in São Paulo and Rio de Janeiro. The decline was even greater compared with the real value of the wage at the end of Kubitschek's government. As the incomes of working class families fell, more and more women were obliged to go out to work, often taking over jobs previously almost exclusively the province of men, such as street cleaners, bus conductors and bank clerks. This development had profound effects on both the political role of women in Brazilian society and their place inside the family.

Another important feature of the boom was the expulsion of large numbers of rural workers from their jobs. This process was brought about under legislation introduced during Goulart's term of office and strengthened by Castello Branco, which gave rural workers the right to the minimum wage and some social benefits. Rather than raise wages to the legal minimum and contribute towards the cost of the social benefits, landowners and farmers laid off their workers on a massive scale, and diversified away from labour-intensive crops like coffee into mechanized crops like soya or extensive activities like cattle breeding.

Expelled from the land, thousands of unskilled rural workers flocked to the large cities like Rio de Janeiro, São Paulo and Belo Horizonte. Finding ready employment on building sites, they provided the labour for a colossal boom in construction as early as 1968. For accommodation they had only slums and the shanty towns (*favelas*), which mushroomed at this time. When they looked for new jobs, it was usually in manufacturing, which expanded rapidly in the 1968-73 period.

These were the key years of the 'miracle', when the whole economy, fuelled by cheap oil, was booming. Gross domestic product rose from US$52 billion in 1963 to US$134 billion in 1978. The most dynamic sectors of industry were dominated by multinationals, including the whole of the motor industry, electronic household goods, and most of the plastics, pharmaceutical and tyre and rubber industries. From 1968 to 1974, gross domestic product grew by an average yearly rate of 10 per cent, more than double the rate of growth of advanced countries and well above the rate achieved during the Kubitschek administration.

The increasing number of goods that were produced were consumed

The Jari Project

The most glaring example of the invasion by multinational corporations of the Brazilian countryside was that of the Jari project. In 1967, Daniel K Ludwig, one of the world's richest and most secretive entrepreneurs, bought 3.7 million acres of land in the Amazon basin, and planned to spend US$700 million in the first phase of various extractive and industrial activities. Amongst the projects were:

● the cornering of the world paper market. This involved the removal of the natural forest, the planting of trees (a species of which is noted for its rapid growth), and the building of enormous pulp and cellulose plants.

● the development of the world's largest rice paddy. Covering 30,000 acres, its target production was 100,000 tons per year by 1980, made possible by planting high-yield Filipino 'miracle rice'.

● the largest palm tree plantation in the world. With 60,000 acres under palms and on-site processing facilities, production of palm oil and special lubricants was envisaged.

● exploitation of the unexpected deposits of kaolin, or white clay, used in the coating of paper. Reserves of 40 million tons were discovered.

● large-scale ranching. By 1973, Ludwig had placed 15,000 cattle — mainly buffalo — in Jari, aiming to raise this to 50,000 by the late 1970s. The plan was to export processed meat to European and North American markets.

● other crops — such as soya, sugar, manioc, corn and castor oil — were planned, complete with processing facilities.

● the Jari area is also rich in bauxite, diamonds, gold and tin. Ludwig hoped to finance the entire project through the development of these resources for export.

Although encouraged by the Brazilian government, Ludwig's project attracted criticism and opposition from almost every other quarter. The secrecy under which the project operated, the mounting of a private security force around its perimeters (giving rise to accusations of Ludwig operating 'a state within a state'), the exclusion of 'unauthorized' journalists, the ecological alteration of a vast stretch of the Amazon, the vulnerability of the Apalaí Indians, the growth of huge shanty towns immediately outside the area and the high level of exploitation of the workforce — all served to gain the project worldwide notoriety, despite the government's attempts to whitewash it internationally.

By 1979 it was running its own police force, schools, hospitals, port and airport. It applied its own liquor laws and the port collected no customs duties. There was no control by the Brazilian authorities. The issue of sovereignty gained such prominence that incoming ◗

President Figueiredo felt obliged to send his Interior Minister, Mario Andreazza, to the area. Andreazza took with him a party of journalists and drew up his own itinerary rather than submit to Ludwig's escorts. The result was the setting up of a commission to consider Jari's future.

In 1980 the losses arising from the project amounted to US$75 million, and conflict developed between Ludwig and the government over who had responsibility for the provision of social services and infrastructure. These factors, and the likelihood of defaulting on loans (according to SNI), led to Ludwig transferring Jari to a Brazilian entrepreneur, Augusto Trajano de Azevedo Antunes.

Antunes put up 40 per cent of the private capital, and with government help, pressurized a group of 23 bank, finance and construction companies into purchasing equal shares of the remaining private stock. The new Companhia do Jari was inaugurated in January 1982, faced with Ludwig's debt and all the other problems associated with the project.

Marcos Arruda, 'Daniel Keith Ludwig', in *Multinationals and Brazil,* Toronto, 1975; *Financial Times* 13 and 20 July 1979, 8, 15 and 22 January 1982; *Relatório Reservado* 791, 11-17 January 1982.

by a fast-growing and prosperous middle class. During the first half of the 'miracle', it was this market that gave industry the base from which to launch its products onto the world market in the second half. The whole system of national savings was geared to financing the durable and capital goods industries, and middle class consumption. The new middle class also provided the personnel to run the modern new factories, and to staff the state apparatus and the financial system. To cope with the increased demand for engineers, doctors, economists, journalists, and so on, higher education, traditionally the state's responsibility, was opened up to private capital. As private high schools, colleges and universities mushroomed, the number of university students climbed from 278,000 in 1968, to almost 800,000 in 1974 and over one million today.

It was the car that dominated the life-style of the middle class at this time. Consumption, living, leisure, urban geography, transport, all were determined by the car. This period coincided with the heights of the political repression, and many cars carried the famous slogan issued by the authorities: 'Brazil, love it or leave it'. The squeeze on working class wages allied to the rapid growth in middle class salaries obviously led to a further distortion in the distribution of income. The proportion of total income going to the poorest 5 per cent of the economically active population fell from 1.51 per cent in 1960, to 0.54 per cent in 1972. The share of total income of the poorer half of the population fell from 15.87 per cent in 1960 to 10.49 per cent in 1970, then recovered somewhat to 12.94 per cent in 1976. The increased share of the richer half was taken almost entirely by the richest 10 per cent, whose slice of the cake grew from 41.28 per cent to 51.15 per cent.

During the boom years, 1968-73, Brazil's exports increased from less than US$3 billion to just under US$10 billion. Leading the export drive was soya, which in the early 1960s had hardly been cultivated. Sensing the potential of such agricultural products, the government subsidized the purchase of farm machinery and inputs such as fertilizers. The agricultural sector became a leading consumer of industrial products and export earner, even as it shed a significant part of its workforce. Exports of manufactured goods (shoes and machinery), and processed goods (cocoa products) and minerals also grew. Coffee lost its dominant role among exports, accounting for just over 10 per cent of earnings in 1974 compared with almost 40 per cent in 1968.

Crisis of Succession

The major crisis during this period occurred in August 1969, when President Costa e Silva suffered a heart attack on the eve of signing the new constitution which he had sponsored without much support from the rest of the army. It was intended to pave the way for the re-opening of Congress, which had remained closed since the decree of Institutional Act No.5. Whether Costa e Silva's stroke was the result of the tension produced by the widespread resistance within the military to the new constitution is not clear, but Costa e Silva retired from the presidency and died shortly afterwards.

He should have been succeeded by the civilian Vice-President Pedro Aleixo, who had opposed Institutional Act No.5, but instead the army high command installed a junta consisting of the three armed forces ministers to run the country while the question of how to deal with the succession was discussed.

The high command, which is dominated by the commanders of the four armies, and also includes four chiefs of services, all four-star generals, and the army minister, took an unprecedented decision: to choose the new president after formal consultations with all the army generals, air force brigadiers and navy admirals. A majority of the 120 votes in the air force and navy went to General Albuquerque Lima, the leader of the right-wing army nationalists. But heavy pressure was put on electors not to vote for Albuquerque Lima, and in the end the majority of army votes was given to General Emílio Garrastazu

Médici, a former head of the National Intelligence Service, SNI.

Taking over from the junta in October 1969, Médici presided over both the years of the miracle and the worst repression. His term of office also saw the introduction of censorship on a number of important daily and weekly publications.

5 After the 'Miracle'

Double Shock

In 1974, two events deeply shocked the Brazilian dictatorship: the tripling of oil prices and the massive vote for opposition candidates in elections to the Senate. With the new price of oil an era of glorious capitalist expansion that had reached its apotheosis in the 'Brazilian economic miracle' came to an end. With the spread of the protest vote the political system, created by the military to ensure that its own party always won, finally turned against its creators.

Early in the year, when President Ernesto Geisel came to power, accompanied by his *eminence grise,* General Golbery do Couto e Silva, the regime had apparently been working like clockwork. A 'new class' of military and civilian technocrats, at home in the giant new state enterprises, was the increasingly central locus of power. The working class had been successfully eliminated as a political protagonist, and within the dominant strata, so long as the boom lasted, there was room for everyone. Potential antagonisms, it seemed, could easily be bought off. Why not, then, go for the final prize of international respectability, by removing the cruder aspects of dictatorship? And this, indeed, is what Geisel and Golbery proposed to do.

Geisel and Golbery personified authoritarian military technocracy. Their background was not in active service, but in the National Intelligence Service (SNI), which Golbery himself had founded. Immediately before assuming the presidency Geisel had commanded, not troops, but the state oil company, Petrobrás. His inauguration signified a return to power of the group of military 'intellectuals'

Abertura's Eminence Grise

General Golbery do Couto e Silva was one of the key ideologues to emerge from the *Escola Superior de Guerra* — the Higher War College — in the post-war period. He was a key figure in designing the *abertura*. He left public office in August 1981 after acting as head of the president's civilian household — a chief advisory position — under both Geisel and Figueiredo. Prior to that he had been instrumental in setting up the *Serviço Nacional de Informações* (SNI), Brazil's intelligence agency. His downfall opened the way for the hard-line faction, under General Octávio Aguiar de Medeiros, SNI's present head, to gain ground. However, Golbery is attempting to block Medeiros's presidential ambitions for 1985 and to back those of Colonel José Cavalcanti, head of both Eletrobrás (the state power company) and the Itaipú hydroelectric project.

For many years Golbery's ideas also provided the theoretical framework and rationale for Brazil's foreign policy. In July 1980, *Latin America Regional Reports: Brazil* questioned Golbery's role in the light of changes in the trend of Brazil's external relations.

'Men of all latitudes and all races, take heed: war is global', General Golbery warned in 1952 at the height of his cold war fervour. During the next two decades he retained his belief that international relations were determined by an all-out war between the 'democratic west', headed by the United States, and the 'communist east', dominated by the USSR. It was Brazil's role to participate actively in this war, and, more specifically, to assist Portugal in carrying out its 'African responsibilities' by helping to combat the independence movements in its colonies.

These chauvinistic views, which contrast markedly with the non-ideological profile of current foreign policy, were expressed in General Golbery's famous book, *Geopolítica do Brasil*, first published in the early 1960s. At the same time, he published his ideas on domestic issues, particularly planning and national security, in a collection of essays, *Planejamento Estratégico*.

While Golbery's early views on domestic issues have remained highly pertinent, his ideas on foreign policy have suffered a different fate. They were extremely influential during the first military government, under General Humberto de Castello Branco (1964-67). Foreign policy was summarized by the then foreign minister, Juracy Magalhães, in the famous phrase: 'What is good for the United States is good for Brazil.' Golbery not only drew up the overall policy guidelines but also helped to carry them out. For instance, he himself travelled to the United States in 1965 to arrange for Brazil's participation in the US intervention in the Dominican Republic.

Golbery fell from grace during the Costa e Silva and Médici

◆

governments (1967-74). On his return to power in 1974, he found that important changes in both world and Brazilian politics had rendered his geopolitical views absurdly anachronistic, though Brazil's foreign policy had stagnated.

In the following years, foreign policy changed decisively, whether Golbery approved the changes at the time is not known: the major tenets of his previous position were, after all, turned on their heads. The old anti-communism was reserved strictly for domestic use; abroad it was replaced by pragmatic trading relations with both Soviet bloc countries and the People's Republic of China. The Third World was recognized and afforded a status that had been lacking before, and the former special relationship with the USA was further down-graded by the creation of a 'European option'.

Latin America Regional Reports: Brazil, RB-80-06, 4 July 1980.

gathered around Castello Branco in the early years after the coup — the *castelistas* — and opened a gap between the presidency and those forces in the army most deeply compromised in acts of repression.

At his first ministerial meeting, in March 1974, the new president announced that the 'exceptional executive powers' which characterized the regime as a dictatorship, might be eliminated by the end of his term of office. But it was an extremely cautious announcement: 'We will sincerely direct our efforts towards a gradual, but safe, democratic improvement.' The dictatorial powers which he insisted were essential to secure the country's social and economic development, 'without dangerous interruptions or set-backs', he hoped to see less and less in actual use, until eventually they might be replaced by the 'effective, constitutional safeguards' characteristic of a strong, highly centralized, bourgeois democracy. This was the project of *distensão* or political relaxation with which Geisel became identified. Its emphasis was less on change, than on an institutionalization of the *status quo*. Already, however, the leap in oil prices was generating tensions that would cause the reassessment of this project.

The End of the 'Miracle'

The Brazilian economy, more than any other, epitomized the oil age. Since the time of Juscelino Kubitschek, the country's entire industrial and transport infrastructure had been developed on the assumption of cheap petroleum. The motor car was not only the spearhead of a new cycle of industrial expansion; it was also the crucial status symbol of the new middle classes. The increased bill for fuel imports, coupled with the effects of recession in all the major Western economies, put paid to this rapid expansion. The growth in the gross domestic product (GDP) fell from 14 per cent in 1973, through 9.8 per cent in 1974, to the historically low figure for Brazil of 5.6 per cent in 1975. The balance of payments was thrown into long-standing deficit, due to the already enormous outgoings of hard currency, a result of the very high level of foreign capital investment in the country. The deficit on current account, which is a measure of a country's dependence and the amount it needs to borrow just to go on taking part in world trade, jumped from US$1.5 billion in 1972 to US$6.7 billion in 1974. Five years later, despite a twofold increase in export earnings, it stood at US$10 billion per year. The total foreign debt passed from US$5.3 billion in 1972, through US$12 billion in 1974, to US$45 billion in 1980 — the largest foreign debt ever carried by any country in the world. The economic 'miracle', which had been nothing other than a colossal expansion of productive forces on the basis of wretchedly cheap energy and labour, as well as on more capital-intensive technology, was over.

A Breach in the Alliance

Geisel and his technocrats were slow to admit what was happening. The industrialists were not. They were worried about who would bear the burden of diminishing economic growth. In particular, they were concerned at the preponderant role of the highly profitable state enterprises, over and against the private sector, in the process of capital accumulation. They feared, for example, that to protect its own fiefdom the government might take protective, even 'nationalist', measures, such as restricting the remission of profits to parent companies abroad, clearly to the detriment of the large private industrial groups. A vigorous campaign was launched, not against Geisel, but against state intervention in the economy, led by Eugenio Gudin, the doyen of reactionary economists and Brazilian representative of the Chicago School, exponents of strict control of the money supply in order to control inflation. Such ideas have been applied by right-wing governments under the influence of Milton Friedman and other Chicago University economists. Simultaneously a campaign was launched against multinational corporation. FIESP, the powerful São Paulo industrialists' organization, played a key role in both the anti-statist and anti-multinational initiatives.

This campaign turned into the Brazilian capitalists' first big political operation independent of the military, precipitating an uncertain rift in the pact between the armed forced and industry. As the economic crisis developed, and the tensions between different factions intensified, the political implications became clearer. Unable to re-establish a global consensus within the existing order, industrialists began to demand readjustments in the form of the state itself. Or, as they themselves put it, they wanted an enlarged space for 'dialogue', in which their particular interests could be expressed more forcefully.

As an extraordinary congress of the major employers' organizations stated later, in 1977:

this project (of economic and social development) can only be achieved with a desirable degree of political freedom, in a pluralist, multiple society, and insofar as economic power is decentralized.

The Protest Vote

The disintegration of any consensus in society at large had been brought home most forcefully at the elections of November 1974. An electoral system designed to acquire the stability of the Mexican system, where one party dominates the political sphere, had turned into a plebiscite against the government. In the election of federal deputies, where the traditional machinery of local patronage is stronger, the government party, ARENA, held on to a greatly reduced lead. In the elections to the Senate, however, the tables were turned. The opposition party, MDB, received 14.5 million votes, against 10.1 million for ARENA. Since only some of the senate seats were in dispute, this did not give the opposition a majority. It did, however, remove the government's two-thirds majority, which Geisel would have needed to get passed his planned changes in the constitution. Worse still, it indicated that when further senate seats came up for election in 1978, ARENA would almost certainly lose even its simple majority, thereby giving the opposition power to veto legislation going through Congress.

In part this turnabout at the polls had to do with the growing disaffection of the new middle classes in the face of recession. It also had to do with the fact that for the first time the radicalized grass-roots church communities, the CEBs, and most of what remained of the left after the decimation of guerrilla struggles in preceding years, had begun actively campaigning for the MDB. And it was helped by the opposition campaign's skilful use of its limited access to television, by now installed as the predominant mass medium, reaching virtually every corner of the country and every layer of society.

But more than anything else, it reflected the profound

transformations undergone by Brazil's social structure in the preceding decade and a half. The opposition's support was concentrated in the big urban centres.

With millions of peasants and labourers being evicted from the land by the mechanization and concentration of agriculture, the urban centres had grown incredibly. In 1960, only 45 per cent of the population lived in the towns. By 1970, the balance had been inverted: 59 per cent lived in the towns, surpassing 60 per cent before the middle of the decade. By 1980 the proportion would reach 68 per cent. Contrary to the Maoist dictum is was the towns that were surrounding the countryside.

The capitalization of agriculture also meant that staple food crops were increasingly supplanted by export crops like soya. The supply of food per urban inhabitant fell by 30 per cent between 1965/7 and 1974. Prices rose, and wages fell behind. In 1974 a worker needed to work 157 hours to earn enough to buy the 'essential minimum ration'; ten years earlier it would have required just 100 hours' work. The need for more breadwinners per family led to child labour almost doubling in five years. Public services like transport and sanitation virtually collapsed in the overburdened towns. Epidemics of polio and meningitis killed thousands in the early 1970s, with children especially vulnerable. 42 million people were estimated to be living in extreme poverty, whilst the extreme wealth of the top 10 per cent was greater than ever.

For the military, the most obvious solution to the deteriorating electoral fortunes of ARENA might have seemed simple: put a stop to elections. But this option appeared too dangerous. Instead, Geisel and his team began to look for ways of maintaining the façade, by changing the rules of the game. The idea of 'institutionalization' took on a new and much more urgent meaning, rather different from its initial one.

The Return of the Military Hard-liners

Another threat to Geisel and Golbery's project came from the extreme right in the armed forces. At the end of 1973, even before Geisel took office, the repressive machinery had begun to stir against the promise of *abertura*. Already engaged in eradicating, so far as possible without traces, the rural guerrilla base set up in Araguaia by the PC do B (the Chinese-line communist party), the hard-liners began to kidnap and summarily execute the leaders of other remaining left-wing organizations, including the VPR and the ANL, and, in April and May 1974, the PCB itself. This last move, the elimination of members of the Communist Party Central Committee, was a clear warning shot across Geisel's bows. For unlike the other groups, the communists had opposed armed struggle, with their policy of support for gradual and careful liberalization, had up until then been relatively spared from repression.

Arrests and torture continued with renewed ferocity in subsequent months. The crunch was precipitated in October 1975 when Vladimir Herzog, an extremely well-known journalist who worked at TV Cultura in São Paulo, died under torture while being interrogated by the army about his alleged involvement with the PCB. The army claimed he had committed suicide. São Paulo's intelligentsia expressed its outrage at his memorial mass with an eight thousand strong demonstration — the first the country had seen for many years.

Whilst the public clamour continued, Geisel publicly maintained his support for General Ednardo D'Avillo Mello and his fellow hard-liners in command of the Second Army in São Paulo. At the same time, he began to manoeuvre his own men into key positions. When, in the following January Manoel Fiel Filho, a metalworker, died in almost identical circumstances, President Geisel was ready to move. He immediately sacked General Ednardo, and dispersed his crew. Taken by surprise, the Army High Command bowed to the president's authority. For the time being at least, the hard-liners had been outflanked.

In the meantime, the government had already begun to tune up the instruments it felt it needed to deal with the parliamentary opposition. In April 1975, on the pretext of removing a corrupt official in the remote territory of Rondônia, Geisel had resuscitated the most potent dictatorial power of all, the notorious but long-unused Institutional Act No.5 (AI-5), which gave the president almost unlimited individual powers to intervene in any aspect of the political or administrative process. The same powers were used twice again that year. The incidents involved were unimportant, but the principle of such intervention had been re-established.

In January 1976, immediately after sacking General Ednardo, Geisel again resorted to AI-5. In the course of two months he suspended the political rights of five of the MDB's most vociferous deputies, partly to mollify the hard-liners in their discomfort, and partly to warn off the opposition. The municipal elections due in November 1976 would provide a measure of the need for further political reforms. In June the right of political parties to use specified hours of airtime on television for their electoral propaganda was rescinded. ARENA would naturally benefit, given the pro-government colouration of the usual television coverage.

The government did not feel directly threatened by such local elections, where the traditional machinery for 'buying' votes worked even more effectively than in national and state assembly elections. In the event, ARENA candidates succeeded in most small towns. But the MDB's support had doubled since the previous local elections in 1972, and the administration of almost all the industrial towns now passed into the hands of opposition mayors and councils. Grave surgical measures were obviously essential for the government to avoid disastrous defeat in the senate elections due in 1978. These measures came in April 1977.

The April Package

On the carefully engineered grounds that the opposition was obstructing a bill to reform the judiciary, President Geisel again resorted to his exceptional powers. He used AI-5 to close down Congress and to impose by decree the constitutional adjustments which would legalize these actions and subsequently enable him to do away with those same exceptional powers, including AI-5 itself.

These reforms, elaborated by Geisel, Golbery and their intelligence chief, General João Baptista Figueiredo, tucked away in the president's country residence of Riacho Fundo, became known as the 'April package' *(pacôte de abril)*. Its most important component was the measures to reinforce the regime's control over Congress. The provision for a two-thirds majority required to pass constitutional amendments was replaced by the need for only a simple majority. To prevent the opposition from ever using this to approve its own amendments, separate votes would be made compulsory in the Assembly and the Senate. To ensure the government's control in the Senate, a special category of senator, not elected but nominated by a safely government controlled electoral college, was instituted. The opposition quickly dubbed this new category the 'bionic senators', after a popular American television hero, the bionic man, partly reconstructed after an accident, making remote control of his actions possible.

Another series of measures aimed to adjust the electoral process in ARENA's favour by giving greater weight to the more easily dominated rural areas. The number of representatives from each region would no longer be calculated according to the number of voters, but according to the number of inhabitants. This was intended to favour country regions where the concentration of those illiterate, and therefore without voting rights, was supposed to be highest. In fact, this particular measure backfired. Unforeseen arithmetical complications, together with the fact that huge numbers of the

59

illiterate had now been forced to migrate to the towns, meant that this measure ended up actually increasing the weight of the opposition's urban strongholds. Almost symbolically, this isolated, self-styled constituent assembly of three had got its sums wrong, and had failed those of its supporters who certainly would have spotted the error.

Other measures included extending the ban on using television for electoral propaganda, re-affirming the system of indirect election for state governors, and extending future presidential terms of office from five to six years. At the same time the choice of presidential successor by electoral college was moved forward to the October before taking office — in other words, one month before the general elections which might unfavourably upset the composition of the electoral college.

Institutionalizing the Regime

The April package gave Geisel the framework in which to recycle the regime's system of power. The first step was to impose his own choice, General João Baptista Figueiredo, to succeed him as president in March 1979. Figueiredo was not an immediately impressive candidate, but he was a loyal pupil of the Geisel-Golbery school who, as an ex-head of President Médici's military household, also had good relations amongst the factions represented in that previous governmental team. Furthermore there was some disquiet about his sudden promotion by Geisel to the rank of four-star general, which elevated Figueiredo's presidential chances above those of a number of hard-line hopefuls. Even so, he was not popular with many troop commanders, and his 'election' by electoral college depended on circumventing a series of challenges from within the system.

The most dangerous of the challenges came early on. Long before Geisel's choice was officially announced, the hard-line army minister, Sylvio Frota, had begun to preen himself for the succession, openly opposing liberalization, defending fidelity to the 'revolution' (the military's code word for the 1964 *coup)*, and gathering his support amongst those sectors that had felt humiliated and insulted by Geisel's dismissal of General Ednardo. More worryingly still, both Geisel and Frota knew that it was these hard-liners, schooled as colonels in the counter-subversion of the late 1960s, who in the normal course of promotion were about to supply a majority of the army's generals. On 12 October 1977, Geisel took the unprecedented step of sacking his army minister, simultaneously moving with dexterity to neutralize his potential support and thereby avoid the very real threat of a counter-*coup*.

In the wake of this averted crisis, a series of lesser dissident currents, of varied ideological persuasion, began to form in the armed forces. None of these acquired much political weight in their own right, but several of them did come together around another alternative presidential candidate, the supposedly nationalist retired general Euler Bentes. His campaign eventually developed into the National Front for Redemocratization, with the official backing of the MDB. Capable of drawing crowds of up to 15,000 at its rallies, the Front seemed at first to pose a real threat. But it was fatally flawed by a complete absence of political coherence. Spanning the gulf between liberals, extreme right-wing nationalists, the left-wing *auténticos* in the MDB who favoured substantial reforms, and a number of unabashed careerists from within the regime's ranks, its only real common ground seemed to be a deep dislike of the gang that commanded the presidential palace. All but sabotaged by the MDB leadership, it failed to pick up significant support from ARENA malcontents and inevitably collapsed as Geisel successfully steered his own choice through the electoral college in October 1978.

The second and decisive step towards institutionalization was already under way. In June Geisel had published the text of the constitutional reforms which would enable his successor, Figueiredo, to rule without resort to exceptional dictatorial powers. The president would no longer be able, on his own, to suspend anyone's mandate or political rights, to close congress, or to impose any legislation he wanted simply by decree. Instead, the president's control of the normal legislative process would be consolidated, the electoral manipulations already introduced by the April package would be retained, the National Security Law beefed up, and provisions be introduced for a National Security Council, nominated by the president, to be able to declare a State of Emergency that would, whilst it lasted, return to the president just about all the powers he had supposedly lost. The arbitrary powers of dictatorship would not so much be revoked, as built into the constitution.

These reforms, due to take effect the following March when Figueiredo assumed office, were passed by Congress before the November general elections. Although MDB made new gains in these elections, the immediate future of *abertura* from above had already been secured. And in any case, plans were already afoot to split up the MDB opposition by reforming the political parties.

If the parliamentary opposition seemed, for the time being, to have been disarmed, this was not the case in civil society at large. For it was outside the strictly political domain, in the broader reaches of popular movement, that the most serious opposition forces to the military regime had been accumulating. To these we must now turn our attention.

6 The Struggle Unfolds

The Church as Opposition

Within the popular movements no other institution has done so much to expose the military regime over the last decade as the Catholic Church. With 320 bishops, 12,000 priests and 45,000 nuns spread as far as the remotest village, the church has been the only organization capable of steering and building on people's daily discontent on a national scale.

In 1964, the church had given the military *coup* its blessing, even mobilizing sections of the middle class in its support. It is true that some groups, like the Basic Education Movement in the north-east and the Catholic Youth dissociated themselves from this stance adopted by the church hierarchy and soon found themselves in conflict with the military. But it was only after the famous Medellín Conference in Colombia in 1968 which formally aligned the Latin American church with the poor and oppressed, and especially after the murder by para-military groups in the north-east of a priest associated with the work of Dom Helder Câmara, that the clerical hierarchy itself began to turn against the regime. This change was a response to the repression itself. For the first time in Brazilian history, priests were being arrested, tortured and killed.

In siding with the interests of the majority against the policies of the state, the church had discovered a formula for survival in a violently changing society. The ecclesiastical base communities (CEBs), local groups of ten, twenty or even fifty christians meeting periodically, which had existed on a small scale since 1960, spread rapidly after 1965. In 1978 there were between fifty and eighty thousand such communities, guided by lay or clerical 'pastoral agents', and involving some two million people.

The bishops became political as well as spiritual leaders. In São Paulo Cardinal Evaristo Arns was in command of an immense network of human rights activists. In the heart of Amazonia Dom Pedro Casaldáliga was effectively leading the resistance of poor, squatter peasants, the *posseiros,* to the invasion of their land by multinationals and other big companies from the south. In Santo André, an industrial suburb of São Paulo, when police repression was at its worst, Dom Claudio Hummes put the church at the disposal of workers' strike movements.

Commissions set up by the National Bishops' Conference (CNBB) to work in particular sectors — the so-called 'pastoral commissions' — have produced some of the most important studies denouncing different sorts of poverty and oppression in the country. In February 1977, the CNBB issued a manifesto entitled *Christian Demands for a New Order,* containing the church's position on the institutional crisis, a document which took up the most advanced positions of the liberal opposition and demanded a regime of social justice and democracy. In 1979, the CNBB published a balance sheet of its casualties in the virtual war between church and state. It recorded hundreds of cases of churches being raided, death threats and kidnappings. Eight members of the clergy had been murdered and eleven banished from the country; 122 had been arrested, and 34 of these had been tortured. Another 131 lay workers had also been arrested. In the face of repression, the church identified even more closely with the people's struggles.

The church's active presence in the field of popular struggle has been disconcerting and demoralizing to the regime. Contrary to what is stated in the National Security Law, the church understands Christ to be with those who struggle against the government. It is the left, rather than the military rulers, who have seemed to embody national traditions, interests and culture, including catholicism. The government has been cast in the uncomfortable role of anti-Christ.

Moving Back into the Streets

Out of the ecclesiastical base communities was born the first genuinely grass roots movement to occupy an important space on the political scene, the Cost of Living Movement, made up mostly of the poor from the outskirts of the big cities. By the eve of the 1978 elections this movement was mobilizing thousands of people at rallies in many state capitals, a demonstration of the awareness and organizational capacity which these slum-dwellers had already attained. It was the Cost of Living Movement which, together with the student movement, led the fight to win back the streets as an arena for political expression, itself an almost physical measure of the degree of real *abertura,* as opposed to the precarious variety of *abertura* being handed down from on high.

In addition to the slum-dwellers themselves, and particularly the women, the Cost of Living Movement was supported by left-wing activists who throughout this period worked closely with the church. Such collaboration dated from the time when many of them belonged to *Ação Popular* (AP), a Marxist group founded in 1962 by ex-members of the Catholic University Youth (JUC) and the Catholic Student Youth (JEC). The church's role in land struggles produced an affinity with the Maoists as well, whose political strategy attributed great importance to this area.

Early in 1978 a meeting of 5,000 approved the Cost of Living Movement's manifesto of four basic demands:

● an emergency cash bonus of 30 per cent for all workers;

● a price freeze on all basic necessities;

● wage increases in keeping with human dignity of workers and their families; and

● agrarian reform to give the land to those who wish to work on it.

In August, just three months before the elections, members of the Movement's co-ordinating committee walked into the presidential palace in Brasília and deposited petitions containing 1.3 million signatures in support of the four demands.

The Cost of Living Movement not only demonstrated the local base communities' ability to take co-ordinated action on a national scale. It had also begun to undermine the government's machinery of electoral patronage in the localities.

The Rebirth of Student Politics

The student movement in Brazil has a long tradition of supplying the left with many of its leading activists. For that reason the re-emergence of student politics drew down the full rancour of the regime's repression. But the reaction was anachronistic.

The student population at the end of the 1970s numbered over a million, three times that of the early 1960s. But more and more of these were fee-paying students at private colleges who felt little sense of identity with popular struggles. The proportion of student activists had diminished, whilst the new leaders of the popular opposition were increasingly found to be emerging directly out of the shanty town movements and industrial struggles which finally exploded in 1978.

The first big student strike occurred in São Paulo in 1975, but it was not until 1977 that the tension really broke loose. Beginning with a huge march by 10,000 students through the centre of São Paulo, violently set upon by the police, demonstrations quickly spread to other parts of the country. Arrests, injuries, the military occupation of universities, and massive operations to prevent the reorganization of the illegal National Union of Students (UNE), all demonstrated the pathological character of the regime's response. Only at the end of the year did the repression begin to ease off. But such gratuitous police violence against peaceful student demonstrations had done much to undermine the government; it had stoked the fires of middle class discontent which would feed into the amnesty campaigns of 1978.

Eventually, in May 1979 in Salvador, the founding conference of the new National Union of Students was held. The huge numbers present had finally forced the governmemnt to abandon its policy of repression. As far as the students were concerned, not for a single moment had *abertura* been handed down from above; it had been fought for, inch by inch, all the way. And although won in practice, this limited *abertura* has still not been formalized. The government maintained its repressive legislation against students, and still refused to recognize their union, UNE.

The Amnesty Campaign

Alongside the student mobilizations, several sectors of the liberal opposition, including academics, lawyers, parts of the MDB and the National Front for Redemocratization, began to demand respect for civil liberties and the constitutional process. Essentially these were attempts by the elites to repeat the pattern of 1945, whereby Getúlio Vargas' dictatorship had been recycled into the forms of parliamentary democracy, withouth touching the *status quo* in society itself. None of these liberal demands really caught on. However, one formally liberal movement did become the focus for large-scale mobilizations — the campaign for a general amnesty.

The amnesty campaign met an objective need of the various opposition currents, all of them truncated by having members in prison or in exile. Amongst the liberal professions it also met a need to make collective amends for their failure to respond to the persecution of colleagues during the worst days of repression. And the thousands of relatives of the victims provided the campaign with a small army of indefatigable activists. The repression had had the paradoxical effect of creating five or ten new enemies for each one that it had eliminated. At the end of 1977, the idea of an amnesty campaign was gathering momentum. In addition to the political prisoners and the 'disappeared', there were 4,682 people who had been dismissed from their posts and had their political rights suspended (the so-called *cassados)* including teachers, politicians, ex-governors and mayors, diplomats, trade union leaders and civil servants. The total number of exiles was estimated to be 10,000. In an elitist society like that of Brazil, where those active on the left, even the guerrillas, included many children of the ruling class, it was inevitable that, once the ice was broken, abomination of the regime's crimes should spread right into the heart of the ruling system itself.

The first few months of 1978 saw Brazilian Amnesty Committees (CBAs) mushrooming in all the big cities. Supported by the left, the church and the liberals, the CBAs soon proved one of the most efficient instruments for combined action by the opposition forces. Public opinion was profoundly shaken by their campaigns. An avalanche of revelations about torture was unleashed. The famous 'list of 233 torturers' drawn up by political prisoners and published by an opposition paper, *Em Tempo,* which included the names of the system's top generals, the successful law suit brought against the state by Vladimir Herzog's family, and the political prisoners' own hunger strikes, continued to put the military regime in the dock, politically, morally, and even literally. Characteristically, the military themselves reacted with threats about 'the risk to *abertura,* personal intimidation, and manipulation of the judiciary, to prevent the past from being scrutinized.

The question of an amnesty, and of what kind of amnesty, became the focus for tensions associated with a transformation of the regime. The campaign reached its peak at its first national congress, held in São Paulo in November. At the same time, differences within the movement became accentuated. Cardinal Arns, who had provided logistical back-up, took offence at the homage paid by the congress to the memory of guerrilla leaders, Carlos Marighela and Captain Lamarca. Liberals, and most notably the followers of the PCB (with its 'eurocommunist' line) opposed any confrontation with the military which would be provoked by raking over the past. According to these moderates, it would not be possible to obtain political *abertura* by turning the armed forces into defendants. On the other hand, for the majority of those active in the campaign, it would be impossible to guarantee any eventual *abertura* without the crimes of the past and those responsible for them being judged.

The First Strikes

By the middle of 1978, however, another decisive factor had exploded on to the Brazilian political scene. At 7 o'clock on the morning of Friday 12 May the 2,500 workers on the day shift at Saab-Scania in São Bernardo do Campo, clocked in as usual, went to their positions, but refused to switch on the machines. They stood immobile, with their arms crossed and their machines stopped. The first big workers' strike for ten years had begun. It was a new kind of strike, without prominent leaders, without pickets, and without scabs. On the following Monday they were joined by 9,500 metalworkers at Ford. Within ten days similar strikes had reached 90 engineering firms in Santo André, São Caetano and Diadema, the dense industrial belt around São Paulo known as the ABC, the heart of Brazil's motor industry. The strikes spread like an epidemic, to the astonishment of the bosses, the politicians, the government, and even what was left of the organized left within the workers' movement. In the space of two months, half a million workers at some 400 factories in 18 towns in São Paulo state tested their strength in strike action, invariably extracting favourable settlements from their employers. Law No. 4,330, introduced by the military regime in 1964 to outlaw strikes, had in practice been overturned.

The advanced sector of this new workers' movement coincided with the advanced sectors of industrial production — the new factories which had mushroomed overnight during the economic 'miracle'. The vast majority of workers in these factories had never taken part in industrial action of any kind — few knew exactly what a strike was. But the 'miracle' had created all the necessary conditions for strikes to break out. Most importantly, it had hugely increased the concentration of workers in individual plants, and in particular areas.

During the big strikes of the 1950s, and even during the previous strikes under the military regime in 1968, the biggest factories did not employ more than 5,000 workers, and even these were few and far between. By 1978, there were 38,000 workers at Volkswagen alone, and 25,000 at Ford. In the boroughs of the ABC, all of them very close together, there were 210,000 metalworkers.

The same pattern was repeated on a smaller scale in the industrial districts of Minas Gerais, Rio de Janeiro, and in the industrial towns of São Paulo state.

By and large this huge mass of workers on the new production lines, including unskilled workers, was better paid than the rest of the working class in Brazil. In the big car factories half the workers earned between three and five times the national minimum wage; only 5 per cent earned the minimum wage, which in Brazil as a whole was earned by one-third of the working population. Nonetheless, in themselves these wages were still low, in stark contrast with the ostentatious wealth of the mostly multinational companies that paid them. On average they amounted to around US$350 a month, whilst in other countries, for the same job, the same firm would be paying US$2000 a month or more.

During the 'miracle' years, this sector of new industrial growth had provided modest opportunities of social improvement for at least some of the millions who migrated from the utter destitution of the rural north-east. However, despite the absence of strong working-class traditions, built into this new sector were the mechanisms which would facilitate the wave of strikes once the opportunities it offered had contracted.

A telling example is the absence of job security. The companies encouraged a rapid turnover of their workforces, in order to avoid having to pay all their workers the compulsory annual wage increases. Many of the workers themselves chose to change jobs frequently, as they saw the chance of doing better in another factory. The military regime had collaborated with the companies by eliminating from the labour laws the long-standing right to job security after ten years in the same firm. In the process, however, they had eliminated one of the last bonds that tied a large number of workers to their employers.

For the prospect of job security naturally encouraged conservative caution amongst those workers with more than six or seven years in the same firm behind them. Once this prospect went, gone too was a sizeable contingent of workers who would be likely to resist, or simply ignore, any strike movement. At the height of the motor industry's boom in the early 1970s, 72 per cent of workers spent less than a year in the same factory. Losing one's job through losing a strike would not be much worse than the normal run of things. But what really brought to workers the need for strike action was the progressive downturn in the car industry from 1972, and especially after the rise in oil prices.

In 1973, following a slight contraction in the market, some companies cut non-wage benefits like free transport. In 1974, inflation doubled to reach 41 per cent, whilst the government falsified at just 21 per cent the index by which wages were annually adjusted. This index, calculated according to a byzantine formula which only the government could understand, was automatic. The corporate unions 'negotiated' their new agreements with the employers, but the crucial ingredient, the wage increase, could not be other than that stipulated by the government.

At the time, the metalworkers' union in São Bernardo was led by Paulo Vidal, strongly influenced by the economic trade unionism of the United States. One of the substitute members of the executive, however, was Luís Inácio da Silva, known as Lula, a toolmaker at Villares, the son of extremely poor parents from the north-east, and the brother of a union activist close to the communists. In 1974, in a climate of mounting tension amongst the union's rank and file, the São Bernardo Metalworkers Union held its bi-annual congress. This congress approved the São Bernardo Charter, which in addition to denouncing the manoeuvres of government and multinationals, attacked the existing corporate union structures inherited from the Vargas dictatorship and unilaterally proclaimed its own independence from these structures. The following year Lula was nominated by Paulo Vidal as his successor, and subsequently elected president of the union.

In 1976, Lula broke from the tutelage of Paulo Vidal and negotiated his own agreement with the employers, separate from that of the Metalworkers Federation. At this stage the question of wage increases was not dealt with, but Lula did succeed in obtaining several non-wage benefits which the Federation had never fought for, including job security for women workers during pregnancy, and for those called up to do national service.

In 1977, Lula took a step that would lead directly to the strikes of May the following year. He launched a new and different campaign, demanding full compensation for the pay lost by workers since 1974 as a result of falsification of the inflation index. On the basis of statistics published by the World Bank, it was calculated that this lost pay amounted to between 18 per cent and 34.1 per cent of June 1977 wage levels. The campaign for the 34 per cent compensation drew thousands of workers to union meetings which previously had barely been attended by hundreds. It demonstrated the readiness of the membership to fight, and consolidated Lula's leadership. A few months later, at the beginning of 1978, Lula informed the labour courts that his members had no intention of accepting the government's readjustment index. February saw the first congress of women metalworkers in São Bernardo, revealing a high level of political awareness amongst women workers. A series of small incidents followed in the factories, including a few very brief stoppages. Some participants in the women's congress were sacked.

For May Day, organizations on the left, including the 'trade union oppositionists' (the name given to those groups of industrial activists linked to underground political currents) called a 'United May Day Rally' in Osasco. Lula decided not to turn up, claiming the need to mobilize around more concrete issues. Twelve days later the strike at Saab-Scania began.

The small groups of the organized left learnt of the first strikes from the newspapers. Trade union leaders, with the exception of Lula and his nearest colleagues, were also taken by surprise by the stoppages as they spread through the factories. The strikers themselves were starting from scratch, inexperienced, and without recognized leaders in each factory. As they met in the factory canteens to discuss their demands, they were obliged from the outset to reach their decisions democratically — something quite new in the elitist traditions of Brazilian trade unionism.

Under the pressure of the strikes, the employers signed the first collective agreement in the National Association of Automotive Manufacturers (ANFAVEA). In the basement of ANFAVEA, the government intelligence service's tape recorders registered these prolonged negotiations word for word. The negotiations were setting precedents for future relations between the new working class and the vehicle industry, both children of the 'miracle'. After years of neglecting an apparently quiescent working class, the repressive apparatus had a lot of information on which to catch up.

Confrontations and Limitations

The arrival of the working class on the scene displaced the liberals and their proposals for purely political reform from the centre of the state. The most developed expression of liberal opposition, the National Front for Redemocratization, had not even included the right to strike in its initial manifesto. In July, Lula attacked the Front, and for the first time suggested the possibility of forming a political party of the workers:

I'm against the National Front for Redemocratization because I think it's a good deal too broad for the workers' tastes. It would be utopian to believe that a front of this sort, initiated by the elites, could respect the workers' right to participate. . . . either the workers make a stand that is coherent with the principles of the working class, even to the extent of creating their own party, or we spend the rest of our lives being towed along behind events as they happen.

Lula recognized the need to win some political freedoms, if only to allow the workers to organize and make their demands. But he posed as an immediate priority the need for the workers to participate politically as a specific and even leading force.

After their first stunned surprise, the government, the employers, and the *pelegos* (the name given to the majority of union leaders, closely identified with corporationism and the interests of the state), all developed strategies to counter the example of the metalworkers' strikes and the emergencies of Lula at their head. In August President Geisel signed a decree outlawing strikes in sectors 'of interest to national security' and establishing legal procedures to rapidly and severely repress them. The employers drew up measures to expel strikers forcibly from factory premises, thereby preventing the 'arms crossed, machines stopped' style of strike, and obliging the workers to rely on pickets outside the gates which the police could more easily suppress.

Some strikes began to flounder. Sometimes this was a result of trying to copy too literally the metalworkers' tactics in quite inappropriate circumstances. This was the case in a big strike by bank workers. Others were broken up by straightforward repression, like the strike at Fiat in Betim, Minas Gerais, where police dogs were used to terrorize strikers inside the plant. Others again were simply tricked into defeat by the *pelegos* leading their union. This was the case at the big cigarette factory of Souza Cruz (a subsidiary of British American Tobacco) in São Paulo, where most of the workers were very young women.

Spontaneous enthusiasm was no longer enough to win a strike. Even the metalworkers suffered a setback. A massive strike by 270,000 metalworkers in São Paulo, Osasco and Guarulhos in October came to a confused and unsatisfactory end. Together with the ABC, these boroughs make up the heartland of Brazilian industry. But their problems are different. The São Paulo metalworkers' union, the largest in Latin America, is in the hands of the country's most powerful *pelego*, Joaquím dos Santos Andrade, and the workers are for the most part spread out in much smaller factories than in the ABC. Insufficient co-ordination and the lack of alternative leadership structures allowed Joaquím to negotiate a face-saving agreement with the employers and demobilize the strike movement.

The São Paulo strike demonstrated an inadequate degree of organization which, for the time being, put even successful sectoral or regional strikes, let alone a general strike, out of the question.

7 Figueiredo's Abertura

The circumstances in which General João Baptista Figueiredo became president in 1979 clearly differed substantially from those which marked Geisel's arrival in office five years earlier. Despite the many uncertainties which lay ahead in this period of transition, Figueiredo at least had the advantage of a seemingly radical policy, *abertura,* with which to placate the opposition. In the event the opposition was to prove in many ways implacable: Figueiredo's first two years in office were marked by strikes, an intensification of conflict in the countryside, unexpected intransigence on the part of opposition politicians, and yet more strikes.

Strike in ABC

The first great confrontation with the authorities exploded the day before Figueiredo took office, when 185,000 metalworkers in Santo André, São Bernardo, and São Caetano came out on strike. In contrast to the historic struggle of the previous year, this strike had been carefully organized by the trade unions involved.

The workers' main demand was for a 78.1 per cent pay increase; with inflation in the previous twelve months running at about 46 per cent, they were clearly looking for an increase in the real value of their wages. But the companies, encouraged by the government's promise to use the security forces to defeat the strikers, were also prepared for the confrontation.

In contrast to 1978 the strikers stayed out of the factories. In São Bernardo, their first meetings were held in the union headquarters, but soon they were obliged to turn to the only venue in town large enough to accommodate their vast numbers — the Vila Euclides football stadium, which now became the scene of gatherings of up to 90,000 metalworkers.

Deadlock was soon reached, as the companies refused to negotiate unless the strikers first went back to work. A 90,000-strong strike meeting rejected this proposal, and on the following day the government decreed the 'intervention' of the São Bernardo union, and the removal of Lula and other union officials from their elected posts.

But the authority enjoyed by Lula and his colleagues was proof against such an authoritarian act. Confounding the hopes of both the bosses and the government, the strike continued, with the active assistance of the local church authorities, who made church premises available to the strikers, and the local council, which had been elected on an opposition ticket in 1976. The grass roots catholic groups known as CEBs provided all sorts of practical assistance to the strikers.

The strike soon continued well past the two weeks for which the leaders had originally planned. Dependent on contributions from the public, generous as these were, the situation of the strikers and their families soon became grave. When the companies offered a 63 per cent rise, but no payment for the days spent on strike, Lula decided that the offer should be accepted. He put his case before a mass meeting. The 90,000 workers present, who had been looking for victory and not for compromise, reluctantly accepted it. It was the first important occasion on which Lula had used his influence to persuade the rank and file to make a decision to which they were instinctively opposed.

When the strikers returned to work a few days later, the authorities withdrew the 'intervention' from the union and restored the elected officials to their posts. It was a cunningly timed manoeuvre intended to weaken Lula's support by implying that he had got his job back by colluding with the authorities to end the strike. But the manoeuvre proved abortive: six days after the strike ended, a 150,000-strong May Day rally filled Vila Euclides. Alongside Lula on the platform were leading figures from both the unions and the political opposition. São Bernardo, or the 'Republic of São Bernardo', as government officials were later to dub this hugely popular movement, had become a symbol of the people's struggle against the regime.

Alliance against Lula

The May Day celebrations marked the end of the period of peaceful co-existance between Lula and union leaders linked to the PCB.

Shocked by Lula's audacious proposal for forming a workers' party, which in their opinion could only be the PCB itself, the communist party began to see Lula as its number one enemy, and began to seek alliances through which he might be isolated and his rapid rise to prominence halted.

It soon found willing allies in the persons of the *pelegos*, who were themselves threatened by the mass democracy of the new workers' movement. This alliance was also aided by the MR-8 group, which had previously been active in the urban guerrilla movement but was now politically close to the PCB, and by some sectors of the Chinese-line communist party, the *Partido Comunista do Brasil* (PC do B). It proved effective in opposing and defeating candidates backed by Lula's newly founded *Partido dos Trabalhadores* (PT) in the elections for union posts where the influence of the new workers' movement was still weak. And to provide an alternative to the new movement in the union field, the communists and the *pelegos* set up their own movement, known as *Unidade Sindical* (Trade Union Unity).

But at the same time other militant union leaders joined forces with Lula, creating a solid nucleus in favour of establishing a workers' party. The eruption of the working class onto the political stage also obliged leading industrialists to reconsider their position, in the process closing ranks with the government once more. Conveniently overlooking their recent criticisms of the state's excessive presence in society, they once more came to appreciate the virtues of state authoritarianism and violence which would be put at their service. In this process the small group of 'progressive businessmen' which favoured a modernization of management/union relations was left out on a limb.

Strikes Everywhere

Throughout 1979 strikes continued to break out in all sectors of the economy, not only in anticipation of the *abertura* promised by the government, but also to counter the effect of the accelerating rate of inflation on wages and salaries.

Worst hit by inflation were public sector employees, who, unlike the majority of workers in the private sector, received no mid-year advance on their annual wage adjustment. In March some 82,000 teachers came out on strike in Rio de Janeiro. A month later it was 65,000 municipal workers in São Paulo city whose numbers soon swelled to 250,000 as colleagues in the rest of the state joined them. Civil servants in Rio Grande do Sul also voted to stop work. Even the forces of law and order were not immune to the rash of strikes, with military policemen in Rio de Janeiro and Bahia downing truncheons.

All in all, hundreds of thousands became involved in public sector strikes, which did much to swing public opinion in favour of the strikers and against the government. A number of strikes, including the doctors', took place on a national scale, leading to the setting up of impromptu organizing committees. Others led to the establishment of employee associations, for most public sector workers are not normally members of trade unions. The habit of holding assemblies and meetings spread rapidly, giving practical form to the promised *abertura,* though not that intended by the government. Nurses, bank workers, doctors, teachers, all took action to win back what inflation had taken from them, and in the process ignoring the ban on strikes in the public services decreed by President Geisel only a few months earlier.

The authorities and the business leaders began to look for ways to take the steam out of the strike movement. But in the end they were obliged to resort to repression. Various union leaders were arrested and charged under the National Security Law, and several unions suffered 'intervention'. Violence was used, particularly against less organized sectors such as building workers and bus crews. In August a building worker named Orocílio Martins was shot dead while on picket duty in Belo Horizonte.

In October the metalworkers in São Paulo city and the outlying districts of Guarulhos and Osasco came out on strike. Their union premises were invaded by police and more than 100 workers arrested. A military policeman shot at point blank range a well-known member of the catholic bishops' Workers' Pastoral Commission, Santo Dias da Silva. His murder made a decisive contribution to radicalizing the progressive clergy and demoralizing the government, which was now identified with the murder of workers. Ten thousand mourners gathered to hear mass in memory of Santo Dias.

In November the government introduced new wage regulations, drafted by the São Paulo industry federation FIESP, to put an end to the wave of demands for pay increases. The new law represented a victory for the workers, in that it took the unprecedented step of introducing automatic wage adjustments every six months to compensate for inflation. Moreover, lower-paid employees, including the overwhelming majority of unskilled workers, received proportionately more. But this extra was funded from a cut in the adjustment given to higher-paid workers. Rather than cut into company profits, the new law aimed at a redistribution of income within the working class.

The new law proved effective in reducing the number of strikes. Automatic wage adjustments removed one of the chief sources of grievance among many groups of workers. But it was less successful in eliminating strikes among well-organized sectors with large numbers of workers.

Amnesty for Torturers Too

When General Figueiredo became President in March 1979, the rhetoric of *abertura* reached a paroxysm. The general himself had first had to undergo facial and behavioural transformation, swapping the regulation dark glasses of the intelligence services chief for ordinary spectacles, and his former taciturnity for a certain loquacity. Some authoritarian traits proved impossible to suppress, however, as was evident when he promised to restore democracy in Brazil 'even if I have to do it by force'.

Figueiredo took his place at the centre of the political stage brandishing the banner of amnesty, now also the leading demand of the opposition, and which he himself had promised as the decisive first stage of the process of *abertura*. But forbidden by the military establishment from offering the full, general and unrestricted amnesty called for by the opposition, Figueiredo resorted to the old trick of presenting his project as if it were all that was possible at that moment, a claim backed up by veiled threats of a return to open authoritarianism if a serious attempt were made to widen its limits. Under the terms of Figueiredo's proposal, amnesty was to be granted to:

● those convicted of political offences, excluding the crimes of kidnapping, robbery and violence against persons, even for purely political motives;

● public sector workers and members of the armed forces removed from their posts under the institutional acts; but re-appointment to a post formerly held was to depend on the approval of the relevant authority or the existence of a vacancy.

It was a half-way amnesty, designed to fulfil the government's need to allow former political leaders to return from exile in the expectation that they would disrupt the unity of the opposition, without ever making any concessions to those who had taken up arms against the regime.

The contradictions of *abertura* showed through clearly enough in the official amnesty project. To meet the insistence of all sectors of the military establishment that judicial investigation of the past activities of the organs of repression should be blocked, the project contained two curious clauses:

● amnesty was to be granted to all those accused of crimes 'arising from political offences', a euphemism for torture and other violations of human rights and the law, committed by the security forces in the course of suppressing the urban guerrilla movement;

● a summary procedure was to be created whereby the relatives of 'disappeared' persons could swiftly obtain a 'declaration of absence' (there being no body in these cases, relatives were unable to obtain a death certificate and settle the affairs of the dead person). In this way the government intended legally to bury the unburied bodies of those who had been kidnapped and murdered by its own agents.

In addition to providing a general amnesty for the torturers, and a very limited amnesty for left-wing militants, the project also opened the door for exiles to return — including 22 prominent political figures whose return, the government planned, would lead to the 'implosion' of MDB. Their hopes for such an outcome rested chiefly on Leonel Brizola, the former governor of the state of Rio Grande do Sul and heir apparent of Brazilian labourism. Once restored to legality, Brizola's *Partido Trabalhista Brasileiro* (PTB) would, it was hoped, syphon off a good part of the MDB and even put it out of existence in Rio Grande do Sul. Miguel Arraes, former governor of Pernambuco, was similarly counted on to draw off another section of the MDB.

But for all the scheming that went into the amnesty project, the real intentions that lay behind it were soon laid bare, and the project was rejected *in toto* by all the forces of the opposition, the church and the liberals. Leading churchmen denounced the intention of granting amnesty to torturers, who, unlike the political prisoners, they said, had never been brought to trial, much less convicted.

On the day that Congress was to vote on the project, hundreds travelled to Brasília to demonstrate their disapproval. But thanks to the last-minute support of ARENA 'rebels', and the lack of decisive action by the MDB leaders, the project was in the end passed without amendment. In the process, however, the new government's liberalizing image took a new knock.

MDB Dissolved by Decree

Under the guise of removing restrictions on the formation of political parties, Figueiredo now proceeded to administer the death blow to MDB (and, of course, to ARENA). In the new era of liberalization, it was explained, there was no justification for maintaining the two-party system. Therefore the two parties would be abolished to make way for whatever new parties politicians wished to form. In the event, MDB went quietly, unable to mobilize public opinion against the blow. Its leaders were anyway divided; some of them, seduced by promises of participation in the government in the near future, were already planning a centre party. Moreover, the tendencies with popular support, especially those connected to the church or influenced by Lula, were already thinking of creating a left-wing party under the control of the workers.

But once the two-party system had been dissolved, the government began putting constraints on the 'freedom' to form new parties. The bureaucratic requirements which were now imposed on aspiring new parties seemed intended to prevent rather than facilitate the process. The new legislation echoed the old in allowing only parties upholding 'democracy' and free of any links with foreign entities — in effect, a ban on the PCB. But it also aimed to make life difficult for the budding Workers' Party (PT) by banning parties basing themselves on 'religious creeds, or racial or class sentiments'.

Elections Cancelled

In mid-1980 Figueiredo, president of the *abertura,* became the first president in 15 years of military rule to cancel an election. Following the serious deterioration in the state of the economy during his first year in office, at the end of which inflation was running at 100 per cent a year, the military were certain that *even with the opposition split into new parties* they would lose the municipal elections scheduled for the following November. But instead of abolishing the individual mandates of their most outspoken opponents, as Geisel did on frequent occasions, they simply abolished the population's right to choose.

The process of formation of new parties was at too early a stage, they said, to allow them to dispute the elections. Thus the underhand manoeuvre which had put an end to MDB now opened the way for another manoeuvre of the same kind.

Bemused by their newly-found freedoms to write and say what they liked, opposition leaders played down the importance of the government's manipulative scheming. Leading opposition figures, with their eyes on the state governors' elections in 1982, showed little concern with the fate of 'minor' elections — such sacrifices, they thought, had to be accepted if the rest of the timetable of *abertura* was to be kept to. Such a self-interested attitude was hardly calculated to win the respect of the many thousands involved in the daily struggle of the grassroots movements.

Itamaraty's Twists and Turns

The 1964 *coup* led to the reversal of the 'independent' direction of Brazil's foreign policy, which had been pursued under the Quadros and Goulart administrations. During that time, Brazil had attempted to adopt a neutral, non-aligned role, with strong anti-colonial overtones. Quadros in particular had sought to strengthen ties with revolutionary Cuba, going so far as to decorate Che Guevara at the presidential palace in Brasília.

However the generals set about purging Itamaraty (the Brazilian foreign office) of those who favoured closer relations with Afro-Asian states. During the first ten years of the dictatorship, Brazil subordinated its world-view to that of the United States. In 1965 Brazilian military forces participated in the US invasion of the Dominican Republic. And under the so-called Nixon Doctrine, Brazil played a part in stabilizing the right-wing dictatorships of Banzer in Bolivia and Stroessner in Paraguay. This period also saw renewed support for Portugal and Lisbon's colonial wars in Africa, and a stepping up of relations with South Africa.

When Geisel came to power he faced three external changes: the global oil crisis, the collapse of the Portuguese dictatorship and empire, and the relative decline of the United States' ability to exercise its political and economic power abroad. Geisel, as former head of Petrobrás, was well aware of Brazil's energy needs, and the necessity to cultivate export markets and sources of finance to offset the country's massive oil import bills.

This led to the policy of *pragmatismo responsavel* ('responsible pragmatism'), whereby Itamaraty again sought to improve Brazil's standing in Africa and Asia. Relations with Middle Eastern oil exporting countries became crucial, and Brazil responded by distancing itself from Israel, and providing countries such as Iraq and Libya with light tanks and armoured vehicles. In the same way, West African countries were courted diplomatically. Brazil sought oil supplies from Nigeria, Gabon and Angola, and in turn these and neighbouring countries became significant export markets for Brazilian consumer goods and services such as construction.

In being one of the first countries to recognize the MPLA government of Angola, Brazil used the fact of their common Portuguese linguistic inheritance to forge new ties. This was extended to Mozambique and the other former colonies of Lisbon. The price was a downgrading of formal relations with South Africa, a key factor in blocking any plans for the formation of a South Atlantic Treaty Organization favoured by Pretoria, Washington and the Southern Cone dictatorships, but doomed without Brazilian participation.

The reluctance of the United States to furnish Brazil with nuclear

▶

technology took Geisel to Bonn, where accords were signed for the transfer of West German technology for the construction of a series of nuclear reactors at Angra dos Reis outside Rio de Janeiro. Western Europe proved willing to provide loans and direct investment on a massive scale, allowing Brazil to diversify its sources of finance, and to decrease its dependency on the United States.

Relations with Cuba, China, the USSR and Eastern Europe have increased over the past few years. In the case of Cuba, it is likely that Brazil will play a part in paving the way for the US to resume trade relations with Havana.

Figueiredo's main emphasis has been on improving relations with other Latin American states. He visited Argentina — the first Brazilian president to do so in many years — in order to mend fences with Brazil's traditional continental rival. Brazil's support for the Argentine case during the Malvinas war indicated the success of the rapprochement. In November 1982 the formal opening of the Itaipú dam by both Figueiredo and Stroessner has provided an occasion for the cementing of ties with Paraguay.

Brazil has distanced itself from the extreme cold war mania of the first years of the dictatorship, but this is simply a reflection in foreign policy terms of the country's altered position within the new international division of labour.

The War on Land Squatters

When the factory workers downed tools for the first time in 1978, a silent but much more bloody war had already been raging for years between peasants or rural workers and landowners — the struggle for land. A strange mixture of non-violent resistance and armed struggle took place mainly between land squatters — peasant farmers bereft of legal title to their holdings — and the big companies or farmers intent on taking possession of their land.

The struggle stretches far back into Brazil's history where it forms an apparently unvarying backdrop to the supposedly more important events taking place in the urban centres. From 1975 onwards, however, the nature of the struggle for land changed as squatters turned to more effective means of defending their holdings. Rural workers suffered from the same kind process of land concentration as the peasant farmers; in recent years, many thousands had lost their jobs. In the process they also lost the small plots of land, the produce from which had traditionally helped to eke out their meagre wages, and were reduced to working on a casual basis. But it was the squatters, rather than the newly-created casual workers, known as *bóias-frias,* who spearheaded the struggle on the land.

Between 1972 and 1978, according to information supplied by the National Institute for Land Settlement and Reform (INCRA), 200,000 holdings of less than 25 hectares were swallowed up. Using more flexible criteria, based on the productivity of a holding rather than its size, some 500,000 *minifúndios* (smallholdings producing insufficient even to sustain their inhabitants) were taken over by large landowners.

The land squatters gained the increasing support of the church, which, with its presence even in the remotest regions, became more and more involved in violent land conflicts during the 1970s. In 1975, after conducting a scrupulous survey of land conflicts, a meeting of catholic bishops in Goiânia set up the Land Pastoral Commission (CPT), to carry out in the countryside the work that was already being done in the towns and cities by the Workers' Pastoral Commission. In a short time the church's action had a decisive effect, for the support and protection of a bishop or a priest fundamentally changed the balance of forces in this kind of localized conflict.

This practical example of the church's 'option for the poor' naturally antagonized the government, which tried unsuccessfully to persuade the Vatican to remove Dom Pedro Casaldáliga, the bishop of São Felix do Araguaia and one of the leading figures of the new 'church of liberation', the most radical wing of the progressive church. In October 1976 a hired gunman murdered a priest, João Bosco Penido Bournier, who was accompanying Casaldáliga to the police station in the village of Ribeirão Bonito, in Mato Grosso, to protest against the torture of squatters' wives held there. The gunman's aim was wayward, for his target was intended to be Casaldláliga himself.

From 1978 onwards, the increasing dissatisfaction of rural dwellers led to a growth in militancy. In August of that year the first big strike of rural workers broke out — 12,000 banana workers from the coastal region of São Paulo refused to work. It was 16 months since they had been paid, a situation due, the companies claimed, to the crisis on the world banana market.

In January 1980 the CPT published its first important document defining the position of the church with respect to land conflicts — the document came down fully on the side of land squatters and landless peasants.

In May of that year the rural oligarchy was surprised by the first strike of *bóias-frias,* which broke out among 5,000 workers on the coffee plantations of Bahia. The strike showed up all the difficulties of organizing *bóias-frias,* but also provided pointers to the way in which these problems could be overcome by the trade unions. The strike failed, but was not considered a defeat. It was followed in September by one of the biggest strikes of the period, when all the

250,000 cane-cutters in the sugar cane growing region of Pernambuco downed machetes.

It would be misleading to say that when the struggle in the countryside intensified in 1979 and 1980, the landowners took a formal decision to eliminate peasant leaders, but the fact is that from this time leaders of rural trade unions started to be murdered with remarkable regularity in the most diverse parts of the country. The first to fall was the peasant leader Pedrinho Marceneiro, murdered in April 1980 in Barra do Garças, Mato Grosso. From then on not a month passed without news of some rural trade unionist, peasant leader or sympathetic lawyer being assassinated. With the death in June 1981 of Joaquím das Neves Norte, a lawyer attached to the CPT and the rural workers union in Navirai, Mato Grosso, the number of victims of this policy of assassination rose to fifteen.

Adopting a similar kind of strategy to its amnesty project, the government tried to cut the ground from under the feet of the church by distributing land titles. In 1980, through its trouble-shooting land distribution agency known as GETAT, and other bodies, the authorities distributed 726,000 hectares in sixteen areas of high social tension, often stepping on the toes of the local oligarchies in the process.

But at the same time the authorities began a campaign against the church, bringing into force new immigration legislation which put foreign priests at the mercy of the state. The church lost its powers to bring clergy freely into the country. Despite long negotiations with the authorities to minimize restrictions on foreign priests, it achieved only minor modifications in the government's original intentions.

The systematic elimination of rural leaders signified a tougher stance on the part of the rural oligarchy, traditionally the first to resort to violence to counter advances in the popular struggle. But this belligerent attitude did not automatically spread to the city-based industrialists, bankers, or executives in the multinationals, as had happened in 1964 when the powerful landowners had been the first to take up arms.

But it is undeniable that the struggles in the countryside influenced the reactions of industrialists and the ruling military group towards the substantial advance of the popular struggle on so many fronts.

The Army Occupies ABC

The military rulers ensconced in Brasília knew very well that for their own survival they would at some time have to destroy the most advanced sections of the new workers' movement at its base in ABC.

The Indigenous Brazilians: A Portrait

Four hundred and eighty-two years after the arrival in Brazil of the Portuguese, the country's indigenous peoples are but a miniscule percentage of the population. Once estimated at between five to seven million, they number less than 200,000 today. Most of them are threatened with extinction by the large landowners and the road network which criss-crosses the entire country.

Throughout Brazilian history, one Indian protection law after another has been ignored, starting with the *Leyes Nuevas de Indias* proclaimed in 1542 by the Spanish crown and revoked three years later by Charles V. In 1680 a Portuguese decree recognized the indigenous peoples of Brazil as 'the first occupants and natural proprietors of the land'. Yet this did not prevent the foreign settlement of Indian lands.

The 1946 Brazilian constitution solemnly proclaimed that the indigenous peoples had the right to permanent ownership of the lands they occupied. However, according to the 1967 constitution, Indian lands are considered to belong to the state. The present constitution (dating from 1969) confirms the Indians' rights to permanent ownership of the lands they occupy and nullifies all land deeds within these areas. The second paragraph of article 198 deprives the owners of any such land deeds of all rights to indemnification.

This has opened the way to abuses by the FUNAI (the government-controlled National Indigenous Affairs Foundation) such as the distribution of *certidões negativas* (negative certificates) officially guaranteeing the absence of indigenous groups in a given area, in order to reinstate the land deeds of persons or businesses who do not wish to give up lands that the constitutional provisions would otherwise return to the Indians. The FUNAI, corrupted by local power structures, has produced innumerable *certidões negativas* for lands inhabited for centuries by indigenous peoples.

On 19 December 1973 the president signed Law No. 6,001, the Indian Statute. Article 65 states: 'The executive power shall, within five years, set the boundaries of indigenous lands'. Four years later, the FUNAI began to carry out this work. But the problem today is still far from being resolved. In fact the situation has become considerably worse over the past decade. Since the turn of the century, 40 indigenous groups have disappeared and several others are in the process of extinction. If the Brazilian authorities do not show the political will to resolve the Indians' problems, beginning with the complex issue of settling the boundaries, the true native Brazilians will disappear.

'Um retrato da nossa populaçao indigena', *Porantim* 4, 37 (April 1982), page 3.

Unlike the struggles in the countryside, which though bloody were isolated far from the urban centres, or the public sector strikes, which did not directly hit factory production, the factory workers' movement was potentially capable of challenging the political power centre itself — as a similar movement in Poland was shortly to prove.

The metalworkers in ABC by 1980 numbered 200,000 and together with their families accounted for almost half of the regions 1.8 million inhabitants. They were not only well aware of their potential political power, but also of the need to fight for political change if they were to achieve real improvements. Moreover, their leaders had shown great integrity in resisting the government's attempts to buy them off in 1979.

None of these developments had been foreseen in the scenarios envisaged for either Geisel's 'relaxation' policy *(distensão)* or Figueiredo's *abertura,* even though both of these schemes had attempted to predict all possible eventualities and prepare ready-made responses for them.

Imagining that the workers' organization mirrored their own, the ruling group in Brasília decided that to destroy the new workers' movement it would be enough to destroy their leaders. And the metalworkers' wage campaign in 1980 offered just the right opportunity. Moreover, at this moment the government had pressing reasons to want to squash the workers' movement, for the 'crisis of the miracle' has deepened with the rise in the price of oil from an average $12.40 a barrel in 1978, to US$17.10 in 1979, and almost US$30 by the beginning of 1980.

The workers' movement itself was in need of a decisive victory, both to compensate for the unsatisfactory settlement of the previous year, and to tackle the effects of inflation. Even six-monthly wage adjustments could not keep up with inflation, which was now running at an annual 120 per cent. This time the metalworkers' basic demands went beyond the customary wage claim. They demanded the recognition of shop stewards, twelve months' job security (to prevent the companies speeding up labour turnover, and thus clawing back whatever concessions had been made to the workers), and a real pay increase of 15 per cent, on top of the normal adjustment for inflation.

The strike exploded on 1 April, with the total support of all the workers in ABC, and another 80,000 in six other towns, who put themselves under Lula's leadership. In some of these places, such as Sorocaba, the local union leaders, though unwilling, were forced by the workers to join the strike.

The authorities wasted no time in bringing the strike before the labour tribunal — but to everyone's amazement the judges refused to declare it illegal. Ignored by the workers in practice, the state's antistrike legislation now suffered a blow from within the ranks of its own representatives.

But at the same time the judges stipulated a real wage increase of only 6—7 per cent, barely more than the 5 per cent offered by the companies themselves, and well below what the metalworkers had demanded. They also rejected the demands for recognition of shop stewards and twelve months' job security. The strikers could have accepted the political victory offered by the tribunal's refusal to rule the strike illegal; but gathered in their thousands in the Vila Euclides stadium, where they turned it down. The level of mobilization achieved in the run-up to the strike was unparalleled in São Paulo's labour history, except perhaps by the great anarchist strikes at the turn of the century. Over 300 meetings had been held and a 400-strong wages committee including representatives from all the large companies had been elected.

The companies had been ordered by the government not to negotiate. As the strike ended its second week in deadlock, the labour tribunal reversed its decision and declared it illegal, thus opening the way for state repression. The minister of labour, Murilo Macedo, ordered the 'intervention' of the unions and the removal of elected officials from their posts, but the strikers held firm. On the nineteenth day, a mass meeting of 60,000 metalworkers decided to continue the strike, on which the attention of the whole country was now focused.

On the same day the repression began, under the command of General Ernani Ayrosa, head of the army's chiefs of staff, who had arrived in ABC the day before. Lula and 15 other union leaders were arrested by agents of the Polícia Federal, DEOPS, and the army's secret internal security unit, DOI-CODI.

The action had been carefully planned in advance by the Second Army commander, General Milton Tavares, in the hope of halting the advance of the opposition by resorting to political terror. Tavares' preparations, in fact, went far beyond what was needed to repress the strike. The security forces had drawn up a long list; it included not only trade unionists but five state deputies, various lawyers well known for taking on political cases, and political activists of various tendencies, including some linked to the PCB, even though the authorities were well aware of the communists' opposition to the strike. It seemed that the local military authorities might even have been preparing a *coup* against President Figueiredo, who was, in their opinion, excessively moderate.

But popular resistance made any thought of a *coup* impossible. A mass meeting of 40,000 strikers decided to carry on, but with one new demand added to the list — the release of their arrested comrades. An immense network of support was thrown up, not just in the locality but across the nation. Some 480,000 tonnes of foodstuffs were delivered to the strikers. Churches became focal points for collecting donations and distributing food to the strikers. The strike fund, consisting entirely of donations, reached the grand sum of 14m cruzeiros (US$3.4m). State and federal deputies and senators and other opposition political leaders converged on ABC, physically intervening when soldiers and police attacked the strikers. The government's tactic of snuffing out the strike by arresting the leaders had proved, in the sight of the nation, a gross miscalculation.

In desperation DOI-CODI agents resorted to acts of provocation, aggressively confronting workers and setting fire to heaps of rubbish in the streets. But their activities were fully reported in the press, and the nation read in detail how the supposed guardians of law and order were transformed into the authors of disorder and violence.

Further arrests of strike activists were made, but on 1 May, a month after the strike began, an immense rally thronged the square outside the main church in São Bernardo. The crowd numbered 120,000. The most combative sectors of the political opposition were all represented. After mass was said, the crowd, led by prominent politicians, women and children, marched through the town to Vila Euclides. Any attempt to enforce the ban on rallies and marches was clearly going to end in a bloodbath, and here the authorities drew the line. The forces of repression were withdrawn from São Bernardo; for the rest of the day not a soldier nor a policeman was to be seen.

The strike lasted another ten days. Already, driven by hunger and lack of money, increasing numbers of strikers were drifting back to work, and finally a mass meeting took the unwelcome but inevitable decision to call the strike off.

The strikers had won none of their demands, but in more important ways the victory was theirs. The whole national security doctrine was exposed as a sham, a means of setting the army against the people. And not against isolated individuals or groups, not secretly or discreetly, but in the most blatant way. And the shock-troops of the repression, the DOI-CODI agents, far from finding a ready-made path back into active service, instead found themselves accused of criminal acts of provocation both by society as a whole and even by colleagues among the military.

Conclusion

In the two-and-a-half-years which have passed since the 1980 strike in the ABC suburbs of São Paulo, the balance of forces has changed somewhat, without, however, affecting the underlying divisions within the country.

On the economic front, the country has been suffering one of the most severe depressions in its history, largely because of the growing burden of the foreign debt which has reached US$80 billion. In 1981 the economy showed zero growth, for the first time since the country has kept proper statistics. The indications are that GNP will actually decline in 1982.

The recession has had a heavy social cost. Unemployment has been rising steadily and the country has been experiencing a growing number of bankruptcies. Yet, paradoxically, this sacrifice has not been reflected in any improvement in the balance of payments. On the contrary, the world recession has meant that the government will be unable to obtain the big trade surplus it needs in 1982 and the extreme nervousness on the international financial markets, particularly after Mexico's financial collapse in early autumn, has meant that the big foreign loans which Brazil desperately requires are no longer available.

As a result, it seems inevitable that, despite its obvious reluctance, the government will be forced sooner or later to turn to the International Monetary Fund. In practice, this will change very little, apart from damaging the government's pride. For the government has already prescribed for the country's ills as bitter a medicine as the IMF could possible require. Though the present recession is still biting deeply, there are rumours, no longer denied by the government, that even tougher economic package, including a ferocious wage freeze, is to be announced shortly after the elections.

The recession has imposed its toll on the labour movement, for there has been a marked decline in the level of industrial action since the 1980 strike. However, unlike the late 1960s, the present period of inactivity does not bear the hallmark of defeat. Instead, the movement appears to have made a tactical retreat to await a better moment for an offensive.

In part, the quiet on the labour front has been caused by the electoral fever which gripped the country in the run-up to the elections held on 15 November 1982. Indeed, many members of the *oposições sindicais*, like Waldemar Rossi (see Appendix Two), have criticized the newly emerged *Partido dos Trabalhistas* (PT — The Worker's Party) led by Lula for weakening the labour movement by putting all its energies into these elections. In return, PT members have retorted that, by holding the elections, the government has ceded some political space and that the party must take this chance to expand its activities throughout the country.

Though the government has permitted the elections, it has taken firm action beforehand both to increase artificially the chances of success of the pro-government party, the PDS, and to make sure that, despite the opposition parties gaining a majority in Congress (as they are likely to), they will find that they have little influence over the way in which the country is governed. The government is prepared to let the opposition parties win the elections, but it will not allow them to rule the country afterwards.

However, this does not mean that the elections are a completely meaningless gesture, nor merely a carrot thrown to the people by a manipulative government. Opposition candidates, particularly from the PMDB, which remains the leading opposition party, are likely to win the elections for state governor in nearly all the states in the industrialized south. Though the federal government wields great power over the state governments, it could find it very damaging to its public prestige to be engaged in an open dispute with an important state government. The election results could thus create a serious political crisis for the regime, the extent of which will be revealed well after the results are declared.

At a military level, the continued power of the armed forces' repressive apparatus has become increasingly apparent. On 30 April 1981, a bomb exploded in the car of two military officers outside a concert hall in Rio de Janeiro. A May Day concert was about to be held and it was clear that the officers were going to leave the bomb to disrupt the proceedings. It was the latest of a series of right-wing bomb attacks.

Though Golbery wanted an investigation, the security services demanded — and obtained — a complete cover-up. This confrontation was largely responsible for Golbery's downfall later that year. He was replaced by João Leitão de Abreu, a lawyer closely linked to the military hard-liners. Since then, President Figueiredo has been very careful not to step on the toes on the security forces, whose power remains today the most serious obstacle to any real return to democratic rule in Brazil.

Appendices

Appendix One

The Fight Over Land in the Amazon

The huge Amazon region, which makes up well over half of Brazil's territory and covers an area over 25 times the size of the United Kingdom, has long been neglected by the people in south Brazil. They are mainly concerned with what is going on in the 'triangle' made up of São Paulo, Rio de Janeiro and Belo Horizonte, where most of Brazil's numerous big factories are found. Yet the recent important changes in the Amazon will soon have a profound effect on the lives of the millions of people in the south.

Let us look at these recent developments. Until the 1940s and 1950s, the Amazon was a huge, sparsely-populated region. There were many Indian tribes, most of which had had little or no contact with non-Indians. There was a sprinkling of families, largely of Portuguese and African origin, living as fishermen on the banks of the rivers. And there were occasional patches of more densely populated areas, largely isolated groups of impoverished families collecting latex from the rubber trees which are native to the region.

Most of the population in the region was centred in the river ports: Manaus, which was extremely isolated 800 miles down the Amazon river, with little, except its magnificent opera house, to remind one of the splendid days it had known during the rubber boom at the beginning of the century; and Belém, much more accessible and developed, on the Atlantic Ocean. But in 1950 the whole Amazon region had only four million inhabitants out of a Brazilian total populaton of 52 million.

By then, the Amazon region had begun to be occupied from the east. Thousands of poor peasant families from the north-east, where huge, unproductive *latifúndios* (estates) monopolized the land, began to migrate to the Amazon, in search of land. The families moved slowly, with their small herds of cattle. They were virtually self-sufficient, producing all their food (largely cassava, rice and beef), cultivating cotton to spin and weave into hammocks and clothes and making rough shoes from the hides of their cattle. At most, they sold a few cattle each year to buy salt, coffee, sugar and kerosene.

Inevitably, these families met up with groups of Indians. An old man in Canabrava, a small community of peasant families to the west of the Araguaia river in the north of Mato Grosso, said that when he arrived in the region in 1956 it was completely wild.'Except for us, the only other people in the region were a group of Xavanté Indians. We were scared of them, for they were known to be fierce. But we learnt to understand them. If we went too close to their village, they killed one of our cattle and left it in a conspicuous spot. We respected their warnings and so we never had any problems with them.'

However, in the mid-1960s the government decided that it was time to 'open up' the Amazon and to exploit its mining and farming potential. It undertook an ambitious road-building programme, beginning with the 1,200 mile road from Brasília, the capital of Brazil, to the port of Belém. To attract businessmen from the south, it began a costly tax rebate scheme by which companies could deduct up to three-quarters of their income tax, provided they invested it in the Amazon. Corruption was rife, for many companies bribed the government officials and then syphoned off the tax rebates into their own pockets. From 1966 to 1979, the government gave its approval to the setting up of 358 ranches, with total tax rebates of US$950 million. However, it is estimated that only 90 to 100 ranches ever got under way.

But this was enough to disrupt the life of the region completely. Many of the big new ranches were owned by powerful Brazilian groups: the largest private banking group Bradesco, the civil construction company Cetenco, the fertilizer manufacturer IAP, and so on. A few were owned by transnationals: the Italian Liquigás (recently taken over by the state oil company ENI), the West German Volkswagen, the US Swift-Armour, and so on.

The government built roads so that the ranches could take their cattle out for slaughter and bring in supplies and equipment, which were largely purchased in São Paulo. Private companies began to set up private land settlement schemes by which plots of land were sold at great profit to settlers from the south of Brazil.

The pace of the occupation process thus accelerated dramatically. A new wave of migration began from the south. It was made up of some of the hundreds of thousands of families from the north-east who had migrated down to the south, particularly São Paulo, but had not been able to get jobs in the factories as they had hoped. Many of these families had gone to live in the shanty-towns which had popped up like mushrooms on the outskirts of the big cities. Others had decided to give up the struggle in the cities and to move back to the countryside; but, rather than go back to the north-east where they knew life was extremely tough, they had opted for the Amazon, encouraged in the early 1970s by the massive government propaganda about the 'March to the Amazon'.

By 1980, the population of the Amazon had risen to 13.4 million, more than three times its level in 1950. Even so, it is still a fairly small proportion of the total population of 119 million.

Real estate offices did great business, selling off vast tracts of land to big landowners from the south. Often these landowners waited until the roads were finished before moving in. When they arrived, they found that patches of their land had been settled on by peasant families who had received no guidance from the government as to which land was really available for them.

Rather than go through lengthy legal procedures (which might even end with a ruling in favour of the peasant families), many of the cattle companies bribed the local authorities to turn a blind eye and sent in gunmen to evict the peasant families illegally. Some unfortunate families found themselves evicted two or three times in seven or eight years. One peasant farmer commented: 'Everywhere I have gone I have planted fruit trees, but I've always been evicted before I've been able to eat the fruit'.

In recent years, the families have begun to resist eviction. They have been exhausted by the upheavals and have become aware that land without an owner is running out and that, if they leave their plots, they may not be able to find another piece of unclaimed land. More and more peasant farmers have been killed in the conflicts.

The Indians have been through a similarly harsh experience. The ranches have shown none of the peasant families' willingness to fit in with the Indians' way of life. Some groups of Indians have been wiped out by disease. Others have been transferred to an alien habitat. With the assistance of the local Salesian mission, employees from the Suiá-Missue ranch (later to be purchased by Liquigás) took the Xavanté Indians near Canabrava to a reserve several hundred miles to the south. Some of the Indians died as a result of the move and the rest took years to adapt to their new environment. For many years afterwards, Xavanté Indians used to escape from the reserve at the end of the rainy season to go and hunt on their old lands.

Nonetheless, many Indian groups have shown remarkable resilience and an impressive capacity to overcome traditional inter-tribal hostilities and to unite in the common cause of the defence of their lands. They have shown that for them the most dangerous period is the initial contact, when they have neither physical resistance to disease nor political awareness of what is happening to them. Many of those who have survived this difficult phase have later shown a surprising ability both to defend their tribal way of life and Indian identity and to adapt to new circumstances.

Perhaps because of their isolated way of life, peasant families have proved if anything more vulnerable to eviction than the Indians. Only isolated groups of peasant families have managed to resist successfully the attempts from cattle ranches to evict them. They have only managed it when groups of families have worked very closely together and when nearly all of them have shown tremendous determination to keep their lands, even if it has meant dying for them. The Catholic church has provided many of these peasant families with invaluable support.

Paradoxically, the great pace at which the Amazon has been developed is beginning to create political problems for the government. For many years, the Amazon has operated as an escape valve for the country's social problems.

The pressure has not built up for the government to carry out programmes of agrarian reform in over-crowded regions such as the north-east and the extreme south, because the landless peasant families have been able to move out and settle in the Amazon.

Moreover, the Amazon has provided the government with a ready solution to tricky political problems. When in 1981 the government had to find alternative plots of land for the thousands of small farmers who lost their land with the construction of the dam for the huge Itaipú hydro-electric power station it is building with Paraguay, it sent them up to the Amazon. When a serious conflict broke out in 1978 between the Kaingang Indians and small farmers in Rio Grande do Sul, it was able to resettle the latter in a land settlement scheme in the Amazon, and so on.

But soon this easy option will no longer be available. Though there are still millions of acres of virgin forest land in the Amazon, nearly every scrap of land now has an owner. Moreover, more landowners are becoming aware of the danger of invasion and are putting armed guards around their estates.

As a result, many more peasant families will be moving back to the cities. Some of them will have been radicalized by a lifetime of struggling for their plots and will join the mass-based protest movements and the country's only legal working class party, the *Partidos dos Trabalhadores* (PT). At the same time, the government will find it increasingly difficult to defuse tense social problems, created by the country's extremely concentrated land tenure, by simply 'deporting' the problem families to the Amazon.

Appendix Two

Interview with Waldemar Rossi

The Latin America Bureau recently took advantage of the visit of Waldemar Rossi to Europe to question him about current trade union conditions in Brazil. First, we reproduce a short biography of Waldemar.

Who is Waldemar Rossi?

Waldemar Rossi, now 48 years old, began working when he was 10, cutting sugar cane in the fields in the little town where he was born, Sertãozinho, in the interior of São Paulo state.

The second of eight children, he had to help support the family, which included two elderly grandparents. From 13 to 27 he worked as a building labourer.

Rossi came from a practising Catholic family, and he soon became involved in the Catholic Young Workers Movement, JOC. At 27 he was chosen as the regional director which meant moving to São Paulo where he has lived ever since. Three years later he left JOC and went to work as a metalworker because he had come to believe in the importance of developing union organization from the grass roots upwards.

In 1966 for the first time he stood as candidate in opposition to the incumbent president in the São Paulo Metalworkers Union elections.

At the same time he remained as an active church member, and joined the newly formed church workers' movement, known as *Pastoral Operário*.

In the early 1970s political repression worsened, with thousands of Brazilians being imprisoned, tortured, and tried by military courts for opposition to the regime.

In 1974, Rossi was meeting with a group of fellow *Pastoral Operário* workers in a church when police invaded and arrested them. Accused of belonging to a clandestine organization he had never heard of — the so-called Popular Liberation Movement, based in Algeria — Rossi was tortured by being strung up from an iron bar and given electric shocks. He was interrogated for days, held in solitary confinement, and finally released after four months without charge. Charges were only brought against him nearly two years later and he was finally brought to trial in 1978 and rapidly acquitted for having no crime to answer. But the years *sub judice* prevented him from standing as opposition candidate in 1975 and 1978, which he believes was the object of the exercize.

In 1981 he stood in the union election and lost by a narrow margin of votes to the *pelego* candidate Joaquim de Santos Andrade, and the powerful union machinery which Andrade has controlled for 16 years.

In October 1981 he lost his last job in a small engineering firm when the recession made him redundant. He made a conscious choice years ago: 'I understood that I didn't just want to be a spectator of history, but to take part in it'.

Brazil Labour Report, 9 October 1981, pp.2-3.

IAR The independent trade union opposition emerged in the late 1970s. Could you explain why you felt it became necessary to involve yourself in this movement?

WR: I have been directly involved in the Brazilian trade union movement since 1962. There was no other option for me but to get involved in this trade union movement, particularly trying to develop grass roots trade union organization, which didn't exist because of the structure of the Brazilian trade unions. The law didn't give any security or guarantees for the existence of the trade union movement within the company. The trade unions are directly under the tutelage of the state, so they live under a perpetual fear of 'intervention' by the state, not an occasional 'intervention', but a permanent state of 'intervention'. Realizing the absence of the grass roots trade union organization, and in the absence of independent trade unions, I, like many others, got involved in order to try and build up this independent trade unionism. The development in the 1970s has been a direct result of that commitment. For example, in 1966, we began to build up nuclei within the factories, taking up whatever immediate struggles were possible, developing the struggle against the trade union structure that existed, and trying to co-ordinate this activity within the factories, trying to transform the trade unions from within. Gradually the Brazilian working class began to take on our proposals, so that what happened from 1978 onwards was really a result of all that discussion and those local struggles which had been going on in the factories.

LAB: You personally experienced the repression of the Brazilian state. Can you outline some of your experiences, including your imprisonment in 1974?
WR: Yes, obviously as a representative of that trade union opposition, the Brazilian government tried to deal with myself and a number of other comrades involved under the repressive laws. It was somewhat difficult for the government and the repressive forces to harass us in terms specifically of our work as the trade union opposition, or indeed on the other hand in terms of our work with the church. So what the government tried to do, working together with the trade union stooges, the *pelegos,* was to have us denounced within the companies where we worked. The result of this was that during 18 years as a trade unionist in the engineering sector, I lost my job 19 times. On top of this, in 1974, the government planned a pretext for charging us under the National Security Law on the grounds that we were involved in a political movement. In 1978 the government itself was forced to recognize that we didn't in fact have any involvement in an illegal political group. Nonetheless in 1974 we suffered electric shock treatment, *pau de arara* (parrot perch, in which the victim is strapped to and suspended from a pole), and generally being beaten up, and a lot of other comrades went through that experience, not just me. And the repression continues to this day. Every step we take is closely watched, and in fact, I have just lost my job again.

LAB: Given the history of state intervention in the trade unions, and the repressive situation which you outlined, how was it possible for the opposition movement inside the trade union movement to emerge?
WR: It emerged from the awareness of the militant workers themselves. We know from history that this kind of movement doesn't emerge spontaneously, and that led us to realize that it was through the involvement of ourselves and other comrades along these lines of working against the trade union structures that that would develop, although we knew that the state would continue to intervene to repress us. The fact that we know this repression will continue doesn't stop us; it means that we have to discover other ways in which to carry on this struggle without allowing the repressive forces to discover and to stop us. And although many of our comrades suffer this repression, and for example, have lost their jobs many times, that actually meant that new groups, new nuclei, were being formed in new companies as these militants moved on from one company to another.

LAB: What is the attitude of the trade union opposition towards the *abertura?*
WR: A few workers believed in the *abertura* but I think most realized that for the workers the *abertura* never really existed. The best proof of that is in the banning, arrest and subsequent sentencing of trade union leaders in São

Bernardo and Santo André. Even in the political sphere, the *abertura* is a farce because the government is creating the impression that Brazil is becoming democratic, whereas in fact it is merely creating a new structure of domination. Basically, what the government is saying to the politicians is that you can marry who you like as long as it's Maria! For example, recently, faced with the possibilty that the so-called opposition parties might actually beat the government, the government has introduced a new packet of legislation to prevent this. In the end, the opposition wanted to marry Joanna, and not Maria.

LAB: The support of the church has been important to the opposition movement. What forms has this taken?

WR: The fact that a number of worker militants were involved with the church, were carrying on their work on two levels — on the one hand creating opposition nuclei within the factories and at the same time working within the church through the base communities — led the church to realize slowly that it was really very separated from the Brazilian reality. As a result of this discovery and of the repression which the government was exerting on the people, the church realized that it had to begin to take some new steps both in the countryside and in the towns. It realized that its responsiblity in forming the awareness of Christians couldn't merely confine itself to the spiritual area, but had to take on the social areas a well.

LAB: Are you really saying that the initiative came not from the church but actually from the Brazilian people?

WR: Basically, yes. I mean of course that there were always some people within the church hierarchy who had a more open view of things, but the real force which allowed the church to develop in this way came from the popular movement and from youth and various other base organizations which had some connection with the church. Even though a lot of these militants were rejected and sometimes repressed by the church itself, the members of these organizations continued to advance and eventually impose a new vision on the church as a whole. This linked up with the work of one or two bishops in the church who had a much more open view of things and who had been working for some time — people like Dom Helder Câmara, Casaldáliga, and so forth.

All this meant that the church had to choose to work for the benefit of all oppressed groups, including workers and peasants. The discovery of the responsibility of the church in developing the awareness of Christians came at the same time as the experience of the fact that this linked up with the educational practice of the church, that is, a realization that it was no longer a question of the word coming down from on high, but it was the people at the grass roots developing an analysis of the situation based on an assessment of the problems, causes and solutions, the historic process involved, and the possible ways out of the situation. As Christians this links up with their conceptions of faith.

LAB: Having looked at the relationship between the state and the workers' movement on the one hand, and the church and the workers' movement on the other, can I turn to the question of the workers' movement and the employers in Brazil? Do you see this particular class, the employers, as being the major antagonist towards the labour movement?

WR: Regardless of my wishes, the fact is, that as the Papal Encyclical of John Paul II pointed out, there is an opposition of interest between employers and employees and that goes on. Despite many years of struggle of workers against many aspects of their employment, the employers have conceded very little or nothing at all, so that independently of whether I want it or not, that opposition exists. The various attempts to reach some kind of agreement, and to point out that so much exploitation cannot continue, have always resulted in a weakening or a defeat for the working class movement so I really don't think that there can be any kind of compromise or agreement between the two. In fact there was a meeting between Catholic industrialists linked to the Association of Christian Industrialists and Christian worker militants at the Catholic University in São Paulo and it was clear that the industrialists were prepared to do anything except give up part of their privileges for the benefit of the living standards and the rights of the workers. They were saying that they had reached a good agreement with their workers because they were prepared to meet a series of the workers' demands, but in exchange, the workers were going to have to meet a series of *their* demands. So we asked, what other demands have you made of your workers after exploiting them for 17 years? And they didn't have any answer.

LAB: Is it possible to differentiate between employers who are locally based and the multinational corporations in terms of their strategies?

WR: The more international they are, the more difficult it is to attack them. It is perhaps more difficult because they are less personal, but nonetheless, to be exploited is to be exploited, and it comes down to the same thing, whether you are being exploited by a local firm which is just paying the minimum salary at most, or perhaps being exploited by a multinational firm which is demanding such a rhythm, a pace of work, which simply exhausts your physical and political capabilities. Nonetheless, it seems to me that in Brazil, as probably in most Third World countries, the exploitation carried out by multinational companies is even more savage than that carried out by some national and sometimes nationalist local firms. Nonetheless the multinationals themselves are simply one facet of the capitalist system, and it is the capitalist system itself which is bad.

LAB: I would have thought that often the multinational companies were actually able, because they have much greater resources behind them, to pay a bit better and to be a bit 'nicer', whereas local companies are often very hard hit by recessions etc., and can't afford that luxury.

WR: This is not quite the case. If you take the example of São Bernardo do Campo, which is the capital of multinational car firms in Latin America, in 1964 there were four *favelas* or shanty towns; 16 years later, there are 54 *favelas* there. Twenty-five per cent (one in four) of the population of São Bernardo at the moment lives in shanty towns. Eighty per cent of the people of working age in São Bernardo work in multinational companies.

LAB: Why is it that certain businessmen are keen to see the state implement the so-called *abertura?*

WR: I think some industrialists are keen to have a certain degree of *abertura* but none of them want to see an *abertura* which includes the workers' movement because none of them are prepared to make any concessions to it. They are interested in a certain kind of parliamentary political opening which will allow them to deal with their means of exploitation in a slightly different way.

LAB: Has the rise in the opposition workers' movement led to an improvement in material conditions for workers?

WR: I think that immediately after 1978 the opposition movement did manage to succeed in winning a series of improvements in terms of wages; but very soon afterwards, the government and the employers managed to recover their position by a series of measures which included not only the National Security Law but also the high turnover of labour and the effects of the recession, which, although it occurred on an international scale, it was intensified to some extent in Brazil to have a negative effect on the working class. The multinationals are taking advantage in promoting the crisis in order to work through their own method of restructuring the Brazilian production processes. So the situation of the working class movement at the moment is extremely critical, in terms of unemployment. So in addition to the effects of difficulties with wages and unemployment, the movement itself, which came out of the trade union opposition and later the combative trade union leaders, has itself suffered a certain reverse.

LAB: Originally the opposition movement was reluctant to become involved in parliamentary politics. What brought about the change of mind on this question? Why has the movement formed a political party, the PT or Workers' Party?

WR: The trade union opposition itself has nothing to do with the formation of a political party, the PT. The PT was the proposal of a number of combative trade union leaders, and subsequently a number of militants involved with the trade union opposition joined in and supported it. The proposal of the PT given the present constitutional and legal situation, is certainly the most advanced, but that doesn't mean that for the majority of workers who are opposed to the existing trade union structures, the PT is the solution. One should never confuse the most advanced opposition with the solution of the struggle of the working class.

LAB: What are the difficulties of the PT in adopting the parliamentary strategy, and how do you see these difficulties being resolved?

WR: In parentheses, I am not a member of the PT. I think that in these terms the difficulties confronting the PT are the same as those confronting all the other opposition parties, that is to say, the government is not in the least bit interested in these parties being in a position to dispute power. This is particularly acute in the case of the PT because it has a position of much more unqualified opposition to the government. So that with this latest package of electoral reforms which is a repressive measure adopted by the government, in my opinion, all the parties are affected by this but the PT is the most severely affected by it. Because in addition to the obstacles which are placed in the paths of all the parties, there is also the question of the obstacle and bans which it places on the trade union leaders who have been removed from office, which is the case of many of the leadership of the PT.

LAB: In what ways do you differentiate your position from that of the PT?
WR: There are two distinctions. The PT sees itself as a political party representing the totality of popular opposition movements, whereas the trade union opposition is an opposition movement within the trade union movement which sees itself strictly in terms of trade union opposition without any affiliation or link to any political party. Personally, I would prefer to devote my efforts to developing the strength of the various popular movements on different levels, so that they can create organisms which will be organisms of expression of the powers of workers in particular areas, however limited.

LAB: The PT and its allies form one wing of the labour movement. How would you characterize the other wing?
WR: That's not correct. It's not the PT and its allies which form one side of the workers' movement — it's the various movements for independent trade unionism which form the one side of the movement. The experiences of these movements existed prior to the formation of the PT. The fact that a majority of militants in the trade union opposition movements support the PT does not mean that there is an alliance between the PT and the combative trade unionists. In fact, within the trade union opposition movement there is the trade union opposition proper, the combative leaders of trade unions, and other groups within the trade unions who are opposed to the existing trade union structure. On the other side, there are the *pelegos,* the government stooges, and certain sections of the left with reformist proposals, who have made an alliance with them, and which form a current called *Unidade Sindical* (Trade Union Unity).

LAB: What has been the effect of the intervention of Lula, his removal from office, and his subsequent arrest and trial along with other unionists in 1981?
WR: The intervention was completely rejected by the majority of workers to the point where the people put in place of Lula and his comrades by the government were not at all able to stand as candidates for the election. On the contrary the intervention actually served to radicalize the workers of São Bernardo because the workers saw that the government was intervening directly to defend the interests of the employers. I think that the best example of that is the solidarity strike which took place at Ford's as a result of the sentencing of Lula and his comrades. I understand that it wasn't just Ford in fact, but a number of other factories also came out on strike in solidarity.

LAB: Finally, I just want to ask about your visit to Europe. What importance do you attach to it and to the question of international solidarity?
WR: My visit was the result of an invitation from The World Council of Churches to take part in a meeting which happened in Stuttgart of various churches to discuss and question the effects of multinational companies, and at the same time the role of the churches in this situation. Obviously, given the opportunity of coming to Europe, I wasn't going to limit myself to the one big meeting, so that I'm also trying, at the request of my comrades back in Brazil, to extend our contacts with trade unions in Europe and with the solidarity

movement. I think solidarity is something we have to build up and seek out in all facets of the workers' movement. I think that there are a whole lot of aspects that need to be tackled, but that one in particular is the development of links, solidarity links between workers in particular sectors, particular firms operating in different parts of the world. The development of links at grass root level between workers in particular companies operating in different parts could help in the struggle against this kind of exploitation on an international scale.

LAB: How do you see growth of similar independent trade union organizations, for example in Poland and in South Africa, where there is great hostility from the state in each case.

WR: It is confirmation that we are not alone in our struggle in Brazil to build up a trade union independence, and that this is the best way for workers in different parts of the world to establish an independent presence. And it's also the basis for the building of a society based on justice and solidarity.

Appendix Three

Suggested Reading

Miguel Arraes, *Brazil: The People and the Power,* Penguin, 1972.

Marcos Arruda, Herbet de Souza and Carlos Afonso, *Multinationals and Brazil,* Latin America Research Unit, Toronto, 1975.

Werner Baer, *The Development of the Brazilian Steel Industry,* Vanderbilt University Press, Nashville, 1969.

Werner Baer, 'The Brazilian Boom, 1968-1972: An Explanation and Interpretation', *World Development* 1-8 (August 1973), pp.1-15.

Richard Bourne, *Assault on the Amazon,* Gollancz, 1978.

Sue Branford, *War on the Last Frontier: Conflict over Land in the Amazon,* Junction, London, 1982.

Jan Knippers Black, *United States Penetration of Brazil,* Manchester University Press, 1977.

Warren Dean, *The Industrialization of São Paulo, 1880-1945,* University of Texas Press, Austin, 1969.

Peter Evans, *Dependent Development: The Alliance of Multinational, State and Local Capital in Brazil,* Princeton University Press, 1979.

Georges-Andre Fiechter, *Brazil Since 1964: Modernization under a Military Regime,* Macmillan, London, 1975.

Peter Flynn, *Brazil: A Political Analysis,* Ernest Benn, London, 1978.

Celso Furtado, *The Economic Growth of Brazil,* University of California Press, Berkeley, 1965.

John Humphrey, 'Labour Use and Labour Control in the Brazilian Automobile Industry', *Capital and Class* 12 (1980-81), pp.43-57.

Francisco Julião, *Cambão — The Yoke: The Hidden Face of Brazil,* Penguin, 1972.

Robert M Levine, *The Vargas Regime: The Critical Years, 1934-1938,* Columbia University Press, New York, 1970.

Neill Macaulay, *The Prestes Column: Revolution in Brazil,* New Viewpoints, New York, 1970.

Guido Mantega and Maria Moraes, 'A Critique of Brazilian Political Economy', *Capital and Class* 10 (1980), pp.125-154.

Ruy Mauro Marini, 'Brazilian Sub-imperialism', *Monthly Review,* 23, 9 (1972), pp.14-24.

Carlos Marighela, *For the Liberation of Brazil,* Penguin, 1971.

Ronaldo Munck, 'State and Capital in Dependent Social Formations: the Case of Brazil', *Capital and Class* 8 (1979), pp.34-53.

Richard Newfarmer and Willard Mueller, *Multinatinal Corporations in Brazil and Mexico,* Report to the Sub-committee on Multinationals, US Senate Committee on Foreign Relations, Washington, 1975.

João Quartim, *Dictatorship and Armed Struggle in Brazil,* New Left Books, London, 1971.

Ronald M Schneider, *The Political System of Brazil: The Emergence of 'Modernizing' Authoritarian Regime, 1964-70,* Columbia University Press, New York, 1971.

Thomas Skidmore, *Politics in Brazil, 1930-1964: An Experiment in Democracy,* Oxford University Press, New York, 1967.

Alfred Stepan, *The Military in Politics: Changing Patterns in Brazil,* Princeton University Press, 1971.

Alfred Stepan, ed., *Authoritarian Brazil,* Yale University Press, New Haven, 1973.

John D Wirth, *The Politics of Brazilian Development, 1930-1954,* Stanford University Press, 1970.

Journals and Newsletters:

Brasilien Nachrichten, Cologne.
Brazil Labour Report, São Paulo and London.
Brazil Information, Rio de Janeiro.
Brésil de Traveilleurs, Paris.
Latin American Regional Reports, Brazil, London.

Appendix Four

Statistical Tables

Table 1

Real Minimum Wages in Terms of March 1982 Value of Cruzeiro

Index of Real Minimum Wages: 1940 = 100

Year	Real Minimum Wage	Index of Real Minimum Wage
1940	21,125.16	98
1945	14.445.59	67
1950	8.586.55	40
1955	23.831.03	111
1960	21.615.88	100
1965	19.221.49	89
1970	14.855.73	69
1975	12.264.26	57
1980	13.314.18	62
1981	13.651.73	63
March 1982	11.928.00	55

Source: DIEESE, April 1982, Special Edition, Minimum Wage, pp.11-12.

Table 2

Minimum Basic Ration: Hours of Work Necessary

Year	Hours of Work	Index (%)
1959	65:05	100.00
1960	81:30	125.22
1961	71:54	110.47
1962	94:48	145.66
1963	98:20	151.09
1965	88:16	136.62
1966	109:15	167.86
1967	105:16	161.74
1968	101:35	156.08
1969	110:23	169.60
1970	105:13	161.66
1971	111:47	171.75
1972	119:08	183.05
1973	147:04	225.97
1974	163:32	251.27
1975	149:40	229.96
1976	157:29	241.97
1977	141:49	217.90
1978	137:37	211.45
1979	153:04	235.20
1980	157:31	242.04
1981	149.40	229.97

Source: DIEESE, April 1982, Special Edition, Minimum Wage, p.4.

Table 3

Direct Foreign Investments and Re-investments in Brazil, by Country
(in millions of US$)

Specification	USA	West Germany	Japan	Switzerland	Canada	United Kingdom	France	Panama	Luxembourg	Netherlands	Sweden	Netherlands Antilles	Grand Total
DIRECT INVESTMENTS													
1969	443.0	148.4	54.5	120.8	151.2	68.0	27.5	44.5	17.1	7.4	16.1	28.2	1,185.2
1970	526.6	180.4	102.2	219.9	220.0	71.2	31.8	52.9	29.6	21.6	26.2	37.7	1,545.7
1971	543.9	238.2	119.7	227.8	235.7	81.1	39.3	63.3	34.0	33.2	32.7	44.2	1,789.6
1972	656.4	271.8	185.6	346.0	236.0	85.4	43.4	76.3	38.3	40.5	39.3	40.3	2,080.9
1973	999.0	355.8	308.6	339.6	253.1	93.7	67.7	93.6	72.1	52.7	42.3	53.4	2,858.6
1974	1,219.1	514.7	583.5	512.0	278.3	133.4	91.3	124.1	91.1	79.2	55.1	50.0	3,925.1
1975	1,468.6	640.3	817.5	665.8	275.0	167.6	126.0	141.0	129.4	96.3	79.2	63.9	4,902.8
1976	1,825.2	824.9	967.1	725.5	344.4	180.6	156.1	161.7	194.2	120.7	131.0	76.8	6,193.9
1977	2,117.0	1,077.9	1,134.4	767.1	373.8	345.6	213.6	168.9	223.3	150.2	143.8	82.0	7,540.0
1978	2,280.8	1,451.8	1,292.8	972.5	413.6	412.8	299.2	176.7	233.4	177.1	216.8	86.4	8,898.4
1979	2,705.5	1,713.9	1,412.3	1,179.3	403.3	499.7	336.8	197.1	263.8	201.7	236.4	222.4	10,595.4
1980	3,254.8	1,733.5	1,573.5	1,051.1	426.1	561.4	381.2	284.6	309.9	226.5	264.8	234.1	11,994.5
RE-INVESTMENT													
1969	372.6	28.9	0.7	55.2	16.4	41.4	7.2	4.0	0.1	1.0	0.6	34.0	525.2
1970	459.8	72.3	2.9	171.1	40.3	136.7	2.5	13.0	0.1	1.5	13.2	20.8	801.4
1971	552.5	93.2	5.2	253.0	58.4	192.0	90.6	11.8	2.3	2.5	25.0	31.0	1,121.9
1972	615.8	100.6	7.1	288.4	69.3	195.4	121.8	22.0	8.3	27.8	29.7	35.9	1,323.2
1973	718.3	161.0	9.7	129.4	107.0	230.8	137.7	38.4	36.1	43.7	30.9	59.9	1,720.6
1974	803.4	195.0	14.5	232.3	123.1	267.6	150.6	62.9	39.4	74.5	63.8	81.9	2,102.2
1975	826.7	231.1	23.7	278.6	135.8	262.7	174.1	76.5	44.3	88.5	65.7	93.4	2,400.7
1976	1,076.1	293.1	38.8	255.2	137.6	2,400.0	170.1	113.4	58.8	112.9	89.2	1,115.0	2,811.2
1977	1,301.2	455.5	68.9	435.5	145.8	201.0	216.1	184.8	78.6	156.3	89.2	145.9	3,688.5
1978	1,541.3	644.9	110.7	655.3	284.0	331.7	279.9	199.6	94.5	123.4	124.5	158.8	4,842.0
1979	1,669.4	749.3	105.8	742.0	222.2	436.5	339.1	214.5	96.3	148.5	142.8	157.7	5,367.6
1980	1,752.1	714.3	151.5	717.4	214.4	549.9	320.8	217.2	95.1	135.4	148.4	146.3	5,485.6

Source: Central Bank of Brazil

Table 4

The Twenty Largest Corporations in Brazil, 1981
(all figures in billion cruzeiros)

Conglomerate	Control of Capital	Sales	Net Profits	Net Equity	Taxes
Petrobrás	state	2,178.8	80.1	716.3	468.7
Shell	foreign (UK/Neth)	400.0	4.0	50.2	6.0
Siderbrás	state	327.9	(−9.9)	254.1	62.0
Exxon Brazil	foreign (US)	319.8	5.0	28.1	7.2
Souza Cruz	foreign (UK)	280.4	14.1	48.5	224.7
eletrobras	state	269.9	136.2	910.3	22.1
Telebrás	state	248.7	98.6	464.3	34.6
Ipiranga	Braz. private	211.3	2.1	30.2	—
Eletropaulo	state	200.0	28.2	490.5	0.1
Copersucar	Braz. private	196.6	0.0	11.0	11.0
Atlantic	foreign (US)	184.0	4.0	17.0	5.0
Volkswagen	foreign (W. Ger.)	180.0	(−20.5)	34.0	14.6
Ford-Philco	foreign (US)	179.0	1.0	27.0	36.0
Texaco	foreign (US)	177.4	2.6	13.3	20.7
Pau de Açucar	Braz. private	167.5	6.2	33.6	11.1
Votorantim	Braz. private	154.1	14.9	128.1	46.7
Bung & Born	foreign (US)	144.0	10.5	42.7	23.0
Vale do Rio Doce	state	128.6	23.4	182.0	3.5
Mercedes-Benz	foreign (W. Ger.)	127.1	8.5	75.6	—
General Motors	foreign (US)	126.1	(−0.2)	30.8	38.1

Note: Average exchange rate for 1981: US$1.00 = Cr$92.2.
Source: Exame magazine, July 1982.

Table 5

Land Holding Patterns in Brazil

Type of Rural Property Unit	Rural Property Units				Area							
	Quantity (thousands)		Per cent of Total		Millions of Hectares		Per cent of Total		Average Area (Hectares)	
	1972	1978	1972	1978	1972	1978	1972	1978	1972	1978
Minifúndio (small-scale)	2,437.0	2.038.6	72	67.3	46.2	35.6	12	9	19	17
Rural Enterprise	162.8	112.9	4	3.7	35.9	22.7	10	6	221	201
Latifúndio (large-scale, intensive)	787.2	875.9	24	29.0	270.0	313.8	73	77	343	358
Latifúndio (large-scale, extensive)	0.2	0.3	—	—	17.9	31.4	5	8	102,286	118,045
TOTAL	3,287.2	3,027.4	100	100	370.0	403.5	100	100	109	133

Source: *Brazil Information* 1,1, Mayl-June 1982, pg.20.

Appendix Five

The Human Rights Situation in Brazil (1981)

In October 1982 the **Amnesty International Report 1982** *was published. Below we have extracted the entry on Brazil. The two French priests mentioned were sentenced to 15 and 10 years' imprisonment by a military court in Belem on 22 June 1982. Amnesty International has adopted them as prisoners of conscience, claiming that there were irregularities in police investigations, pressure on witnesses to commit perjury, and that the hearings did not meet internationally recognized standards for a fair trial. During 1982 repression also increased against journalists, with Juvêncio Mazzarollo being jailed under national security legislation on 28 September. This follows the sentencing of three other journalists to 1½ years' imprisonment in June 1981.*

Amnesty International was concerned about the growing number of prosecutions of civilians by military courts on charges related to the *Lei De Segurança Nacional* (LSN), National Security Law, which carry prison sentences of six months to 30 years. The interpretation of this law was so broad that manifestations of the right to freedom of expression and association were treated as threats to national security. During the year Amnesty International followed 10 prosecutions involving trade union leaders, Roman Catholic priests and members of the Brazilian congress. A number of journalists were also charged with infringing the press laws for writing articles criticizing military or government agencies. At the end of 1981 more than 20 people faced the prospect of becoming prisoners of conscience.

On 2 September 1981 after protests by Amnesty International and others about the conduct of the trial of 11 São Paulo trade union leaders, the *Superior Tribunal Militar* (STM), Superior Military Tribunal, ordered a retrial. This took place on 19 November 1981 but the military court once again found the defendants guilty of infringing Article 36 of the LSN for their part in a strike in 1980. It sentenced them to terms of imprisonment of between two and three-and-a-half years. A further appeal was lodged with the STM. The defendants had been in provisional liberty since 1980. In December 1981 Amnesty International wrote to the Minister of Justice, Ibrahim Abi Ackel, stating that if the sentences were enforced the organization would consider the trade unionists prisoners of conscience.

In June 1981 a military court in Recife convicted Father Reginaldo Veloso of subversive propaganda and sentenced him to two years' imprisonment. Father Veloso had written a protest song about the expulsion from Brazil in 1980 of the Italian priest Vito Miracapillo. An appeal was pending.

Amnesty International adopted as prisoners of conscience two French priests: François Gouriou and Aristide Camio. They were detained in Belem, and faced possible sentences of eight to 30 years' imprisonment or expulsion from the country if found guilty of "incitement to collective disobedience of the laws". The priests were arrested after an incident on 13 August 1981 in São Geraldo do Araguaia. A man, initially said to have been a farm manager but subsequently identified as a hired gunman, was killed in an ambush by a group of peasant farmers. The evidence against the priests was based on statements from the peasants who accused them of instigating the violence. Cardinal Aloisio Lorscheider, the Archbishop of Fortaleza, stated publicly that the peasants were coerced into making these allegations. There was evidence that some of the peasants had been tortured. Amnesty International believed that the priests were arrested because of their non-violent attempts to defend the rights of the peasants to resist eviction.

On 2 December 1981 Senator Genival Tourinho of the centrist *Partido Popular*, Popular Party, was given a six-month prison sentence, suspended for two years, by the *Supremo Tribunal Federal*, Supreme Federal Tribunal. Senator Tourinho had alleged that senior military officers were involved in organizing a campaign of terror to undermine the *abertura* (the government's policy of gradual liberalization).

Although the judicial death penalty for ordinary offences was abolished in 1979, Amnesty International was disturbed by reports of an upsurge in deliberate killings of arrested criminal suspects by the police. For example, in São Paulo 300 suspects allegedly died in armed conflicts with the police during 1981. In many cases, however, the victims appeared to have been killed after being taken into custody by the police.

In December 1981 the Archbishop of Rio de Janeiro, Cardinal Eugenio Sales, protested that common prisoners in the Ilha Grande prison had been tortured. In late November, following the escape of a prisoner, dozens of prisoners were taken from their cells by the prison guards and beaten and kicked. Some prisoners were allegedly burnt with candles. The prison governor and his deputy were suspended pending the outcome of an official inquiry.

On 2 December 1981 a former prisoner of conscience, Hilario Gonçalves Pinha, was awarded damages for injuries he sustained in April 1975 when he was tortured in the *Departamento de Ordem Política e Social* (DOPS), the Department of Political and Social Order, in Pôrto Alegre. The federal judge ruled that the Brazilian state was responsible for the security and physical condition of its prisoners.